English for the
Fashion
Industry

EXPRESS SERIES

Mary E. Ward

OXFORD
UNIVERSITY PRESS

OXFORD
UNIVERSITY PRESS

Great Clarendon Street, Oxford, OX2 6DP, United Kingdom

Oxford University Press is a department of the University of Oxford.
It furthers the University's objective of excellence in research, scholarship,
and education by publishing worldwide. Oxford is a registered trade
mark of Oxford University Press in the UK and in certain other countries

© Oxford University Press 2012

The moral rights of the author have been asserted

First published in 2012

2016 2015 2014 2013 2012

10 9 8 7 6 5 4 3 2 1

ISBN: 978 0 19 457961 2

Printed in China

This book is printed on paper from certified and well-managed sources

ACKNOWLEDGEMENTS

Sources: p.44 www.uniqlo.com

*The publisher would like to thank the following for their kind permission to
reproduce photographs*: Alamy pp.11 (3/Ruslan Kudrin), 19 (e/PYMCA),
20 (2/Walker Art Library), 22 (Jeff Morgan 09), 23 (wool/Microcosmos),
24 (Ex 2/5/Sergey Goruppa), 29 (a/Picture Contact BV), 29 (e/Dejan
Krsmanovic), 29 (d/Art Directors & TRIP), 42 (david pearson), 44 (GAP/
PhotoEdit), 44 (ZARA/Powered by Light/Alan Spencer), 44 (UNIQLO/
Maurice Savage), 44 (Burberry/Gary I Dobner), 45 (1/foodfolio), 45 (2/
Michael DeFreitas Caribbean), 45 (3/Naturfoto-Online); Courtesy
Boohoo.com/PR Shots p.11 (4); Corbis pp.5 (prototype/Stefanie Grewel),
11 (2 & 5/Condé Nast Archive), 13 (Helen King), 17 (1920s dresses/
amanaimages), 18 (1970s wrap dress/Sean De Burca), 19 (b/Kate
Mitchell), 24 (Ex 2/4/Jim Craigmyle), 28 (SIE Productions), 29 (b/Helen
King), 45 (4/Vladimir Godnik/moodboard); Getty Images pp.5 (design/
Blend Images/Hill Street Studios), 5 (product launch/Thomas Barwick),
5 (retail/Emmanuel Faure), 11 (1/Adam Gault), 11 (9/Steve Gorton),
16 (Round Productions, Inc), 17 (1940s skirts/Walter Sanders), 17 (1950s
full skirt/Chaloner Woods), 18 (1960s miniskirt), 18 (1980s padded
shoulders/Nick Dolding), 18 (2000s skinny jeans/Andrew G Hobbs),
19 (a/WireImage), 19 (c/WireImage), 19 (f/WireImage), 23 (chiffon/
Gunay Mutlu), 23 (satin/Siede Preis), 24 (Ex 1/1, 1/3 & 1/5), 24 (Ex 1/4/Ray
Kachatorian), 43 (ChinaFotoPress), 44 (GUCCI), 44 (H&M/Bloomberg via
Getty Images), 47 (Getty Images North America), 50 (Paper Boat Creative),
58 (group of young people/Ghislain & Marie David de Lossy), 58 (woman
in fur coat/Jens Koch), 58 (a/Jupiterimages), 58 (b/Slyadnev Aleksandr),
58 (c/PhotoAlto/Sigrid Olsson), 58 (d/Paul Bradbury), 58 (e/Jupiterimages),
59, 65 (AFP); iStockphoto pp.11 (6/Jitalia17), 11 (7/Ashley Farland), 11 (8/
Andrey Armyagov), 20 (4/Maciej Laska), 20 (karrapa), 23 (corduroy/
aguirremar), 23 (damask/naphtalina), 23 (lace/Ekaterina Lin), 23 (linen/
Petek ARICI), 23 (taffeta/Plainview), 24 (Ex 2/6/Micah Young); Mary
Ward p.12; Press Association Images pp.5 (manufacturing/An xin/AP),
24 (Ex 2/2/Xu ruiping/AP); Rex Features p.18 (1990s grunge/WestEnd61);
Shutterstock pp.19 (d/Allen Graham – PDImages), 24 (Ex 1/2/paffy),
24 (Ex 1/6/Gordana Sermek), 24 (Ex 1/7/Anton Oparin), 24 (Ex 1/8/Andy
Dean Photography), 24 (Ex 2/1/paul prescott), 24 (Ex 2/3/yuyangc), 55 (1/
K2 images), 55 (2/Mark III Photonics), 55 (3/Gina Smith), 55 (4/Sam Aronov);
TopFoto p.17 (1950s jeans), and (1930s necklass/Roger-Viollet).

Cover images courtesy: Corbis cover (Models on the catwalk/Mark
Makela/In Pictures); Getty Images cover (Fashion designer in studio/
Karen Moskowitz); Photolibrary cover (Fabric in a sewing machine/
Image Source).

Illustrations by: Peter Richardson.

*The author and publishers would like to thank the following for their help and
support in developing the book*: Marion Ward; Lara Aragno, Alberto Iacavoni,
Mario Pellezzari, Elisabetta Brunori, Laura Scamardì, Karolina Gendak,
Elisabetta Passaretti, Gianluca Ghiotti, Alejandro Garza Palomares,
Silvia Schippa, Silvia Vetere, and Daniel Wakahisa at IED, Italy; Rachel
Harraway; Jessica Errington; Marlene McLoughlin; Wendy Artin; Babi
Kruchin and Frances Boyd at Columbia University, NYC; Robert
Anderson, William Mooney, Jeanne Golly, and Charlotte Brown at FIT,
NYC; Jennifer Ward; Janet Carr; Jacki Smith and Theresa Breland at the
New School, NYC; Amanda McGowan; Jill Ward; Jenny Olin-Fox; Paola
Bizzi; Susanna Lisio; Francesca de Caprariis; Nicole Shih-Hui Lee;
Carmen Manzo Warren; Laura Ralph; Rachael Smith; Clare Harrison;
Jane Cotter; Pippa Mayfield.

Contents

About the book

English for the Fashion Industry has been developed specifically for people working in, or preparing to work in, the fashion industry who need to use English every day at work to communicate. The book will equip learners with the language skills and vocabulary necessary to understand typical situations in a fashion context.

English for the Fashion Industry consists of eight units. The book covers many different jobs in the industry from pattern cutter to stylist. It follows the development of a garment from design, through manufacture, to promotion and retail. Units from the book work independently and can be selected according to the needs and interests of the course participants. **English for the Fashion Industry** can also be used for self-study.

Each unit begins with a **Starter**, which consists of a short exercise or quiz and serves as an introduction to the topic of the unit. Practical exercises, listening extracts, industry-specific texts, as well as photos and illustrations help you to acquire key vocabulary and expressions. Each unit closes with an **Output** text followed by questions for reflection and discussion.

When you have completed the whole book you can **Test yourself!** with the crossword on pages 68–69. In the appendix of **English for the Fashion Industry** you will also find the **Answer key** so that you can check your own answers if you are working alone. There are also **Transcripts** of the **Listening extracts** and a **Language test** for each unit.

The **MultiROM** contains all the listening extracts from the book. These can be played through the audio player on your computer, or through a conventional CD player. There is also an **A–Z wordlist** with all the key words that appear in **English for the Fashion Industry** . This includes a column of phonetics and a space for you to write the translations of the words in your own language. The **Interactive exercises** let you review your learning by doing exercises that cover the essential language from the book on your computer. This will be particularly valuable if you are using the book for self-study.

1 Introduction to fashion

Look at the photos showing the stages of garment creation. Match the job titles (a–e) to the photos (1–5).

1 Design

2 Prototype

3 Manufacturing

4 Product launch

5 Retail

a Creative director   c Pattern maker   e Sales assistant
b Machine operator   d PR manager

AUDIO 2

1 Listen to five people describing their jobs in the fashion industry. Match the speakers to the jobs.

Speaker	Job
1 _____	a Textile factory manager
2 _____	b Fashion designer
3 _____	c Stylist
4 _____	d Fashion journalist
5 _____	e PR manager

2 **Listen again. For each speaker, cross out the job responsibility they _don't_ mention.**

1 a dealing with clients
  b working with a PR team
  c creating looks

2 a managing a team of staff
  b organizing publicity events
  c receiving awards

3 a illustrating designs
  b manufacturing textiles
  c presenting designs at fashion shows

4 a discussing products with clients
  b operating machinery
  c making contacts at trade fairs

5 a sourcing fabrics
  b working with different media
  c interviewing other people

3 **Complete the sentences using the words from the box with a similar meaning to the words in brackets.**

> come up with • involves • is responsible for • monitor
> negotiating • networking • sourcing • supervising

1 My job as a stylist _____ many skills, especially communication, management, and creativity. (_includes_)

2 I spend a lot of time _____ staff in my team. I need to make sure they know what they're meant to be doing at all times. (_overseeing_)

3 Alejandro is our PR manager. He _____ the brand's public profile in the media. (_is in charge of_)

4 As a trend forecaster, I spend a lot of time _____ with buyers, designers and textile manufacturers so that I can keep up with new trends. (_developing relationships_)

5 I work as a buyer for a big department store and I'm responsible for _____ good prices with our suppliers. (_discussing_)

6 _____ the right materials for each style is a key part of the design process. (_finding_)

7 Working in the fashion industry means you have to constantly _____ new ideas. (_think of_)

8 I'm the merchandising manager for a high street retailer. One of my key responsibilities is to _____ our fashion lines to make sure they are profitable. (_check_)

DID YOU KNOW?

The CAD (Computer Aided Design) system is often used for architectural and mechanical designs but it's also used to create 3D fabrics and models. The CAM (Computer Aided Manufacturing) system helps textile mills produce garments more quickly.

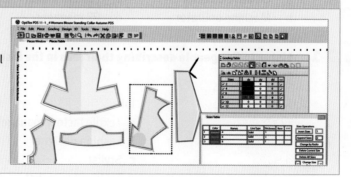

4 Complete the following job advertisements (1–4) with the missing sentences (a–d).

a You will work closely with designers to ensure their designs are translated into well-made garments.

b This will include working on joint projects, such as conducting research to identify client profiles and match them to clothing lines.

c Candidates will need excellent communication skills as they will be responsible for writing print and online promotional literature.

d You will have experience of purchasing textiles and / or any accessories needed for a prototype or capsule collection.

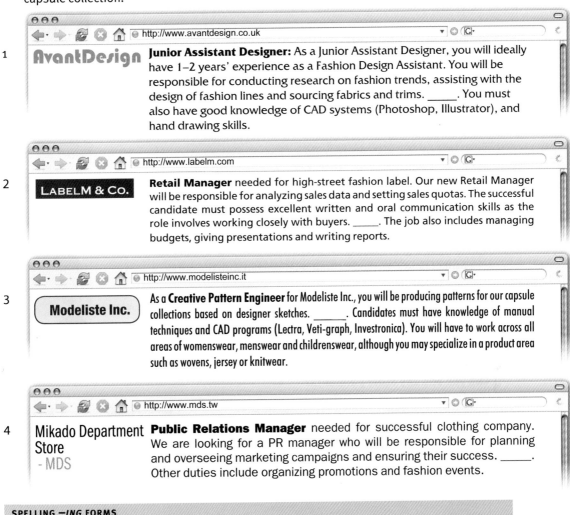

1 **AvantDesign**

http://www.avantdesign.co.uk

Junior Assistant Designer: As a Junior Assistant Designer, you will ideally have 1–2 years' experience as a Fashion Design Assistant. You will be responsible for conducting research on fashion trends, assisting with the design of fashion lines and sourcing fabrics and trims. _____. You must also have good knowledge of CAD systems (Photoshop, Illustrator), and hand drawing skills.

2 **LABELM & Co.**

http://www.labelm.com

Retail Manager needed for high-street fashion label. Our new Retail Manager will be responsible for analyzing sales data and setting sales quotas. The successful candidate must possess excellent written and oral communication skills as the role involves working closely with buyers. _____. The job also includes managing budgets, giving presentations and writing reports.

3 **Modeliste Inc.**

http://www.modelisteinc.it

As a **Creative Pattern Engineer** for Modeliste Inc., you will be producing patterns for our capsule collections based on designer sketches. _____. Candidates must have knowledge of manual techniques and CAD programs (Lectra, Veti-graph, Investronica). You will have to work across all areas of womenswear, menswear and childrenswear, although you may specialize in a product area such as wovens, jersey or knitwear.

4 **Mikado Department Store - MDS**

http://www.mds.tw

Public Relations Manager needed for successful clothing company. We are looking for a PR manager who will be responsible for planning and overseeing marketing campaigns and ensuring their success. _____. Other duties include organizing promotions and fashion events.

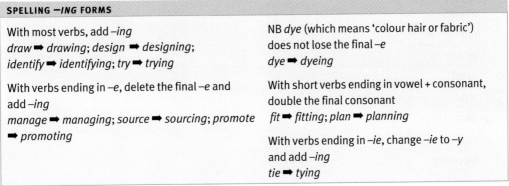

SPELLING *–ING* FORMS

With most verbs, add *–ing*
draw ➡ *drawing*; *design* ➡ *designing*;
identify ➡ *identifying*; *try* ➡ *trying*

With verbs ending in *–e*, delete the final *–e* and add *–ing*
manage ➡ *managing*; *source* ➡ *sourcing*; *promote* ➡ *promoting*

NB *dye* (which means 'colour hair or fabric')
does not lose the final *–e*
dye ➡ *dyeing*

With short verbs ending in vowel + consonant, double the final consonant
fit ➡ *fitting*; *plan* ➡ *planning*

With verbs ending in *–ie*, change *–ie* to *–y* and add *–ing*
tie ➡ *tying*

5 Complete the statements with the *–ing* form of the verbs from the box. Then match the sentences (1–7) with the pictures (a–c).

> analyze • draw • dye • fit • identify • manage • promote • source

1 An important part of the job is _____ design ideas for our womenswear line, either by hand or on the computer.

2 The job involves _____ new trends by doing research on what people are wearing in fashion magazines and blogs.

3 We present our new designs on mood boards. This also means _____ fabric samples for the proposed designs from our fabric library or fabric stores.

4 The _____ process can change how a fabric works, making it shrink or stretch, for example, so our technicians spend time _____ the effects of dye on different fabrics.

5 One of the biggest challenges for a pattern maker is _____ samples for different sizes.

6 As head of the PR office for a luxury fashion brand, I spend a lot of time _____ our relationship with the public.

7 The PR department is responsible for _____ the company's brand through advertising, press releases and events.

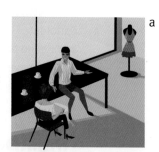
a

b

c

6 Look at the table of garments. Tick (✔) the correct column. Can you add any other garments?

	Top	Bottom	Whole body	Accessory
blouse				
cardigan				
coat				
dress				
gloves				
hat				
jacket				
scarf				
shirt				
skirt				
suit				
trousers				

7   **Label the pictures with the correct words from the box.**

> button • buttonhole • collar • cuff • embroidered motif
> fly • hem • lapel • pocket • seam • waistband • zip

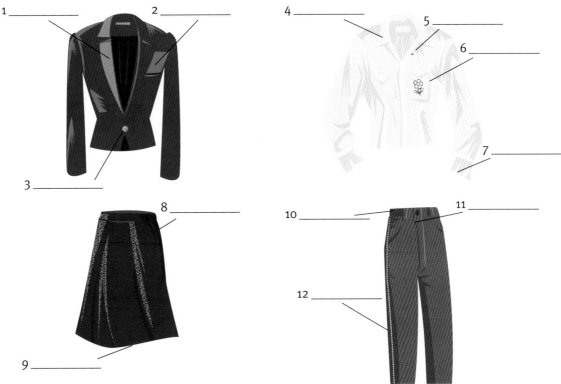

1 _____   2 _____   4 _____   5 _____

                                                        6 _____

                                                        7 _____

3 _____

8 _____   10 _____   11 _____

                                            12 _____

9 _____

AUDIO

3

8   **A designer, a merchandiser and a pattern maker at the Place & Time clothing company are discussing the spring womenswear line. Which garments and parts from exercises 6 and 7 do they mention? There are fifteen items.**

9   **Listen again and answer the questions.**

1   According to the market research, do people like the design ideas for the new line?

_____

2   Why do they decide to focus on the career line in the meeting?

_____

3   How does Erika suggest making the jacket more cost-efficient?

_____

4   What design details are Melissa and the design team thinking of including for
    a   blouses
    b   the coat?

_____

5   What information will Erika know when the sample of the outerwear coat is finished?

_____

10 **Match the colours on the chart with the colour group. There may be more than one possible answer.**

Colour group	Variations
red	
yellow	
green	
blue	
purple	
pink	
brown	

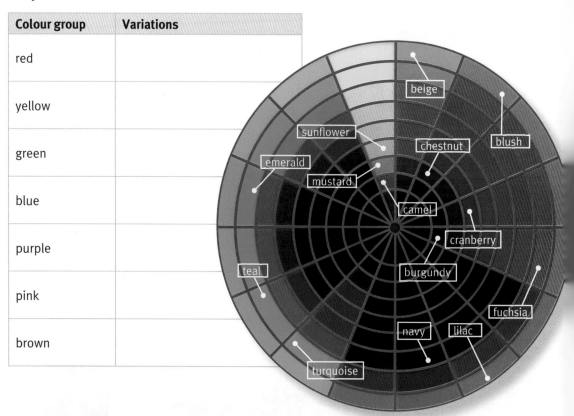

USEFUL PHRASES: DISCUSSING PROJECTS

Asking about current projects
What are you working on at the moment?
How's (your project) coming along / going?
Are you looking into (using) different prints / fabrics?

We're looking into (using fabric buttons).
We're working on (a new line).
We're ready to (give the line a name).
We're thinking of doing (a promotional event).
We're promoting the line with a fashion show.

Talking about current projects
I'm using (pleats) more and more.
I'm doing a lot of research / drawing / sketching.
We're trying to figure out how to (include more prints).
We're researching whether to (use geometric prints).

Describing trends
(More and more) people are buying / wearing (tuxedo-style trousers).
It's / There's a growing trend.
I'm / We're seeing this more and more.
It's becoming (really / very) popular.

11 **Complete the descriptions of the pictures using one item from each box and give the correct garment type.**

Colours

black and white • mustard and black • navy and fuchsia • red and brown • dark grey • multi-coloured • turquoise • green and white • beige and black

Patterns

checked • floral • geometric print • paisley • pin-striped • polka dot • tartan • animal print • striped

1 It's a _____.

2 It's a _____.

3 It's a _____.

4 It's a _____.

5 It's a _____.

6 It's a _____.

7 They're _____.

8 It's a _____.

9 It's a _____.

AUDIO

4

12 **Listen to a designer at Place & Time clothing company talking to a colleague in the merchandising team. Mark the sentences True (✓) or False (✗). Correct the false statements.**

1   Melissa has finished doing research for the new autumn / winter line.   ___
2   The design team is still deciding which prints to use.   ___
3   Prints are unpopular with the company's customers at the moment.   ___
4   They're combining blue and green colours for the line.   ___
5   The PR office is planning an outdoor fashion show for the line.   ___

13 **Listen again. Complete the extracts from the conversation.**

1   _____ to give the line a name: *Blue Turkish Delight*.
2   We're trying to _____ whether to include geometric prints, as well as florals and paisleys.
3   More and more people _____ prints with solid blocks of colour. It's definitely a growing _____ .
4   _____ also _____ some green tones, like teal and emerald.
5   They're thinking of promoting the line by _____ a colour-themed event in-store.

14 **Match the two halves of the sentences.**

1   What are you working   a   into mixing blue and burgundy?
2   The assistant designer is researching how   b   of using pinstripes on the trousers.
3   Collarless jackets are becoming   c   on at the moment?
4   Are you looking   d   very popular.
5   The design team's thinking   e   more and more.
6   We're seeing geometric prints   f   to include prints in the line.
7   How's the project   g   the collection with a big advertising campaign.
8   The company's promoting   h   coming along?

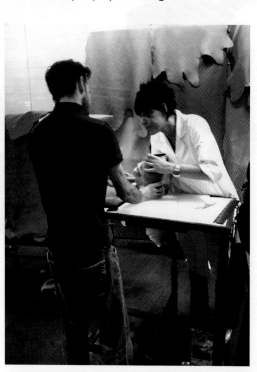

Starting a career in fashion:

Internships, mentoring programmes, and competitions

Internships

People often associate internships with boring tasks, such as getting coffee and making photocopies. However, when an internship is run properly it can be a really fulfilling learning experience. The learning institution, the sponsor and the student sign a learning contract, in which schedules and job duties are defined. Internship duties vary depending on the sector. Students usually work for course credits and are evaluated throughout the semester.

Will an internship lead directly to a job? The answer is not in every single case; it depends on the skills, performance and creativity of the intern. On average, 30–40% of internships lead to a job. In any case, internships offer students hands-on experience in the sector of their choice.

Mentoring Programmes

Designing fashion is an art, but to be a good 'fashion artist' you also have to know how to manage and promote your innovative ideas. Many associations, magazines, and government agencies have initiated mentoring programmes. These are usually aimed at new or recent graduates. Mentoring programmes may support young designers by providing showrooms, pairing mentors to designers, offering workshops on topics like visual merchandising or organizing trips to observe similar work.

Competitions

Various editions of Vogue magazine (US, UK, Italy) have competitions to find bright new talent, run either on their own or in partnerships with government agencies or trade associations. Other associations, such as Malcolm McDowell's and IMG's *Fashion Fringe* in the UK, focus on cultivating talent in the accessories sector. They provide designers with showrooms, where they can show capsule collections to be judged by industry experts. Winners may be awarded paid internships, and many see their creations included alongside major labels at fashion weeks. Some accessory companies have set up their own young talent award projects; Furla in Italy and Aldo shoes in Canada are just two examples.

If you're an extrovert, you may find yourself on a reality TV show such as *Project Runway*, *The City*, or *What Not To Wear*. Winners have great opportunities to launch their careers using the publicity created.

Whatever your area of interest, the fashion industry offers many opportunities to get started in your career.

OVER TO YOU

- What do you know about the following ways of entry into the fashion industry in your country: internships, mentoring programmes, talent contests, or reality TV shows?
- Have you ever participated in any of the learning programmes described above? Which one? What advantages did you gain from it?
- If you have never had an experience like the ones described in the article, which one appeals to you most? Why?

2 History of fashion

How has the fashion industry evolved over the years? Match the key events in the history of fashion (1–6) to the geographical region and time period (a–f).

a England
   1960–present

b Paris
   1800–1950

c Atlantic
   East Coast
   American
   Colonies
   & the
   Caribbean
   1700–1800

d Italy
   (Genoa & Venice)
   1400–1600

e India & China
   1000–1400

f Spain & France
   1600–1700

1 Street-style designs became very popular. _____
2 Marine merchants and traders expanded textile markets and distributed textiles between Asia and Europe. _____
3 North American colonists produced cotton for Europe. _____
4 A new luxury fabric – silk – was invented. _____
5 Haute couture designers, such as Paul Poiret and Charles Frederick Worth, established fashion houses. _____
6 Royal courts created fashion labour rules and laws. _____

AUDIO
5

1 **Listen to a fashion historian talking about some important events in fashion. Put the things she talks about in the correct order.**

Designers & haute couture houses _____

Fashion shows _____

Licensing _____

Sewing machines _____

World expos and trade fairs _____

Department stores _____

2 Listen again and answer the questions.

1 What effect did the use of machinery have on the price of clothing?
2 Where was the first department store opened?
3 What two ways did the House of Worth change fashion?
4 What elements did Elsa Schiaparelli use in her fashion shows to make them more theatrical?
5 What is the modern version of the trade fair for the fashion industry?
6 What did US manufacturers do with licensed fashion labels from Europe?

DID YOU KNOW?

The term 'haute couture', which refers to luxury custom-made clothing, originates from the 'maîtresses couturières' of the seventeenth century. These women were responsible for cutting and sewing garments. While they often had great technical skill, they did not have much influence on fashions. In contrast, modern 'haute couture' is extremely influential on fashion trends.

USEFUL PHRASES

Talking about past events: past simple	Talking about past habits: past simple & *used to*
Who (invented the sewing machine)?	Singers and dancers *used to walk /walked* the runways.
How did (the first designers promote their styles)?	Tights *used to be worn /were worn* by men.
When did (this change)?	There *didn't use to be /weren't* any shopping centres.
The second industrial revolution brought (new fabrics to the fashion industry).	
The couture houses didn't (miss the opportunity to display their creations).	

---

3 Complete the statements using the past simple of the verbs in brackets.

1 Fashion _____ (begin) with merchants trading textiles.
2 When cotton first _____ (arrive) from the American colonies, Europeans _____ (use) it for home textiles.
3 Fashion houses first _____ (organize) fashion shows to promote their designs in the early 1900s.
4 Before department stores, consumers _____ (go) to many different specialty shops to find materials for dressmaking or tailoring.
5 The two world wars _____ (interrupt) the production of clothes.
6 Before the 1900s, designers _____ (not put on) fashion shows.

4 Change the underlined verbs to *used to* where possible.

Although tights and stockings are these days considered to be women's garments, tights were[1] men's clothes before the twentieth century. At first, most tights and stockings were made[2] of wool; silk stockings cost[3] too much for most people to buy. The industrial revolution and mass production made[4] silk stockings more affordable. Before the twentieth century, women didn't wear[5] skirts above the ankle, but changes in fashion put[6] women's legs on display for the first time: hosiery became[7] very fashionable. The invention of man-made or synthetic fabrics like viscose, polyester and nylon after the Second World War transformed[8] women's hosiery. These man-made fabrics were[9] long-lasting and were used[10] not just in hosiery but also for outerwear, home furnishings such as carpet, and even in industrial contexts, as in seatbelts in vehicles.

5 A designer is talking about the influences on their collection. Find and correct three mistakes in the verbs in bold.

I **used to get**[1] my inspiration for my designs this season from 1980s music, you know, new wave, but mostly hip-hop. When music videos **used to appear**[2] on television in 1981, they **influenced**[3] how people dressed. Our collection looks back to that time. Suddenly, young people **used to start**[4] wearing clothes like the musicians in the videos. So, you'll see that our accessories echo the early days of hip-hop when people **used to wear**[5] a lot of gold. But, we also **put**[6] a new spin on hip-hop style jeans by stitching gold embroidery on the back pockets. They **didn't used to do**[7] that. We **refreshed**[8] the hip-hop silhouette by using fitted jeans instead of baggy ones.

1 _____   5 _____

2 _____   6 _____

3 _____   7 _____

4 _____   8 _____

6 Read the description in exercise 5 again. Choose the best word or phrase to complete each sentence.

1 *Get (my) inspiration from* means …
   a find ideas in other places.
   b give ideas to others.

2 *Look back to* means …
   a turning around to look behind you.
   b letting something in the past influence your ideas.

3 If a designer *echoes an earlier style* they …
   a produce exact copies of other garments.
   b use elements of another style in new designs.

4 When designers *put a new spin on* a garment, they …
   a design their own version of it.
   b put embellishments on it.

5 Designers *refresh a look* by …
   a mixing a past style with current trends.
   b using clean vintage clothing in their collection.

DID YOU KNOW?

'Dress' is most often used as a noun to refer to a woman's garment. 'To get dressed' means 'to put on clothes' and 'get undressed' means 'take off clothes'. But in a visual merchandising context, we would use 'dress' as a verb: 'Could you dress the mannequins for the window display?'

7 Look at the timeline of fashion trends. Then match the underlined phrases (1–11) in the text to the adjectives (a–k).

a printed _____
b shortened _____
c tie-dyed _____

d padded _____
e fitted _____
f pleated _____

g layered _____
h ripped _____
i cinched _____

j turned up _____
k dropped _____

Women's Fashion Trends Through the Decades

1920s

Dresses changed a lot in this decade. They became shorter, and they had <u>low</u>[1] waists.

1930s

As Coco Chanel became more fashionable, women imitated her style of wearing <u>lots of</u>[2] long pearl necklaces.

1940s

Women became more practical because they worked while men were soldiers in WWII. <u>Folded</u>[3] A-line skirts became very popular.

1950s

Dior's New Look became popular: a full skirt that fell to just below the knee, and a jacket with a <u>pulled in</u>[4] waist. Meanwhile, American teenagers often wore <u>rolled up</u>[5] blue jeans.

1960s

This decade introduced a more modern – or mod – look compared to the 50s. In London Mary Quant designed miniskirts – skirts where the hemline was <u>above the knee</u>[6]. Hippies wore T-shirts that were <u>multi-coloured using a specialized dyeing technique</u>[7].

1970s

Women started to wear <u>decorated</u>[8] wrap dresses.

1980s

Women's careers became very important to them. They wanted to look powerful in offices to compete with men, so they started to wear jackets and dresses with <u>big</u>[9] shoulders.

1990s

Musical groups such as Nirvana and Pearl Jam made 'grunge' popular, and people copied their style of plaid shirts and <u>torn</u>[10] jeans.

2000s

Many people started wearing <u>skinny</u>[11] jeans with all kinds of footwear: trainers, flats, or high heels.

USEFUL PHRASES

Past participles can be used as adjectives to describe trends or styles. Regular past participles are formed by adding *–ed* to the infinitive:
mix ➡ *mixed*
Many people today wear mixed looks: a tailored jacket with ripped jeans and heels.

There are many irregular verbs:
wear ➡ *worn*
Many people like their jeans to have a worn look.
tear ➡ *torn*
He wore a torn shirt and black leather trousers.

8 **Complete the sentences with the adjectives from exercise 7. Then match the sentences about trends to the correct images.**

1 Last weekend's trend report had photos of many celebrities wearing _____ cuffs on their jeans, also showing great shoes.
2 At the red carpet event, instead of evening dresses, many women chose to wear _____ trousers with a tailored jacket, heels and jewellery.
3 One of the key features of the punk look is _____ jeans.
4 Printed tops with _____ waists and skinny jeans became very popular in the 90s.
5 Last season's autumn / winter collections got their inspiration from the 80s with _____ shoulders and strong shapes.
6 Some summer lines recently included _____ skirts in a rainbow of colours.

AUDIO
6

9 **Listen to an interview with a fashion historian about fashion illustration. Tick (✓) the types of illustration she mentions below. Two types are not mentioned.**

1 painting ☐
2 engraving ☐
3 wood block printing ☐
4 pen and ink drawing ☐
5 hand-drawing ☐
6 silk screen printing ☐
7 computer generated illustration ☐

10 **Listen again. Underline the correct phrase in italics.**

1   Fashion illustration *nearly disappeared / became very popular* after the introduction of photography.
2   The Spanish and French royal courts circulated society papers with *printed / engraved* illustrations.
3   Paul Poiret *paid artists to make illustrations of his designs / got inspiration for his designs from artists' illustrations*.
4   Two artists who contributed to *La Gazette du Bon Ton* magazine often used *prints / wood blocks* for their illustrations.
5   From the 1930s, Vogue used illustration much *more / less* than photography.
6   An advertising campaign for an American store at the end of the last century used *photography / illustration* very successfully.
7   Today fashion publications use *all kinds of / limited types of* illustration.

11 **Match the illustration techniques from the box with the definitions 1–5.**

> computer generated illustration • engraving • hand-drawing
> • mixed-media illustrations • silk screened

1   With a carving tool, the artist creates a picture in a metal or copper plate. They then roll ink onto the block or plate and press it on paper to leave a print. _____
2   The artist uses pencil, pastel, paint or ink to create images on paper. _____
3   This is a combination of different techniques, such as digital and manual illustration. _____
4   The artist uses software to make new designs, such as collages of photos and paintings, or even to create illustrations that look hand-drawn. _____
5   The artist creates a stencil, which is then placed on a frame. Ink is added, and then transferred to paper or cloth. _____

12 **Label the illustrations with a technique from exercise 11.**

1   _____   2   _____   3   _____

4   _____   5   _____

13 Read the email from a fashion magazine editor to an artist. Complete the email with the words from the box.

detailed • drawn • engraved • generated • mixed

From: Camilla D'Arby
To: Jane Rathbone
Subject: Illustration commission

Hi Jane,

We'd like to commission two illustrations from you for our holiday issue. Please have a look at the brief below and then let me know if you have any questions about it.

Illustration 1: An evening gown. We want it to have a soft, elegant, look, so we would like to use an _____ [1] illustration.

Illustration 2: A headshot with jewellery. This image should be _____ [2] media. It needs to be a photograph of a model wearing jewellery with some computer _____ [3] images and hand _____ [4] lines 'traced' on it. It should highlight all the intricate features of the jewellery in a very realistic style, so the illustration needs to be quite _____ [5].

I look forward to seeing your designs!

Best wishes,
Camilla

14 Read the reply from the artist. Match the questions with the editor's responses (a–e) below.

From: Jane Rathbone
To: Camilla D'Arby
Subject: Re: Illustration commission

Hi Camilla,
Thanks for the brief. There are a few questions I'd like to ask:

Illustration 1
1.   How wide would you like the margins for the first illustration?[1]
2.   How detailed would you like the facial features?[2]
3.   Should I make it look like an old-fashioned illustration?[3]

Illustration 2
4.   How big should the image be?[4]
5.   How much of the photo should include computer graphics?[5]

I should be able to finish the illustrations within a week from receiving answers to my queries.

Best wishes,
Jane

a   The illustration should cover half the page. _____
b   The image has to fill the whole page, so just 5–10mm. _____
c   About 30% of the image. _____
d   Yes, we'd like something that echoes art nouveau fashion illustration. _____
e   They should be quite realistic. _____

OUTPUT

The 1920s Cocktail Dress: A reflection of women's rights

The way society expects women and men to behave has been reflected throughout history in the style of dress. The late 1800s are commonly referred to as the Victorian age, after Queen Victoria of England. During this period there were many restrictions on women's behaviour and consequently on the clothes they wore. Socializing mostly took place at teatime in private homes, or outside at tea houses. At these events women often socialized only with other women. They wore long tea gowns which were specifically designed to 'protect women's modesty'.

However, at the same time women's rights movements were starting up all over the world, demanding more rights, such as the right to vote, own land, or earn the same pay as men. As a result of one of these campaigns, women in the United States won the right to vote in political elections in 1920, and British women in 1928. This new-found political freedom was reflected in fashion, most notably in the invention of the cocktail dress. It was designed to be worn at 'cocktail hour' (in the early evening between 6.00 and 8.00 p.m.) and the dress was fashioned to be a stylish garment with a look halfway between daytime and evening.

Beaded Elegance is Decreed for Evening Occasions

Without doubt the most successful of all cocktail dresses was the 'little black dress' (or LBD), which Chanel and Patou are credited with designing in 1926. Two of its most distinctive features were its shorter hemline and black colour. The original design also included a matching hat, shoes and short gloves.

One group of women in the 1920s expressed their new political rights through fashion: the Flappers. Always ready to break society's rules, Flappers went to cocktail parties, moved energetically to dances such as the Charleston, drank alcohol, cut their hair short and had jobs. As the years went by, new, more liberated styles emerged on the cocktail party scene: Dior's shorter dresses of the 1950s, or Galitzine's palazzo pyjama trousers, and Pucci's one piece suits in the 1960s.

Fashion was ready to celebrate women's rights with style and to go with women into a new, liberated era.

OVER TO YOU

- What other social movements have been reflected in fashion?
- Do you think men and women no longer have any restrictions on their clothing choices? Why, or why not?
- In the past 100 years, how much have attitudes changed towards women's clothing in your country?

3 Textiles

Look at the pictures of different fabric types. Answer the questions.

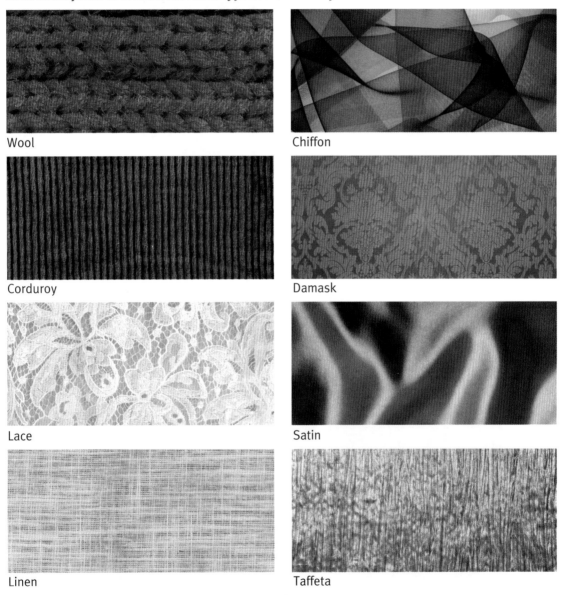

Wool

Chiffon

Corduroy

Damask

Lace

Satin

Linen

Taffeta

1 Which fabrics are most common in spring / summer lines?
2 Which are most common in autumn / winter lines?
3 Which are most common in eveningwear?

1 Label the pictures with the fabric types in Starter. There may be more than one possible answer.

_____ _____ _____ _____

_____ _____ _____ _____

2 Match the stages in the textile manufacturing process with the pictures.

a embellishing _____   c refining _____   e finishing _____
b spinning _____   d dyeing _____   f weaving _____

3   **Listen. Put the stages in exercise 2 in the correct order.**

4   **Listen again and complete the extracts.**

1   First, the raw materials have to be _____.
2   The seeds and leaves in natural materials like cotton need to be _____ so they don't go into the final textile.
3   Next they are ready to be _____ into yarn or thread.
4   Once the yarn or thread is ready, the material is _____ into fabric rolls.
5   After that, the fabric may be _____ – either dyed or printed.
6   Finally, the fabric may be _____ or decorated.

USEFUL PHRASES: EXPLAINING THE SEQUENCE OF A PROCESS

When we describe a process we often use the passive: *Fabric is made from raw materials.*	First / To begin with … Second / Then / Next / After that … Before the fabric is (dyed), it is (woven). At the same time … Once / When the fabric has been (woven), it is then (dyed). Finally / In the last stage …

---

5   **Complete the description of the dyeing process using sequencing words from the Useful Phrases box. There may be more than one possible answer.**

_____ [1], large vats of water are prepared and the dye is mixed.
_____ [2] the dye mix is ready, it is added to the water. _____
_____ [3] the fabric is dyed, a small sample is tested for colour fastness. _____
_____ [4] all of the fabric is dyed, and _____ [5] it is dried,
sometimes in a drying machine and sometimes in the sun. _____ [6],
embellishments are added, when requested by the clients.

6   **Correct the errors with the passive in these sentences.**

1   T-shirts are often *weaved* from cotton or a cotton / polyester mix.
2   Before cotton is *spinned* into yarn or thread, it is cleaned and sorted.
3   Graphic T-shirts are *embellishing* with images, which can be printed or applied with a transfer.
4   Cotton can be naturally *died* using vegetable or herbal dyes.
5   Sometimes several lab dips are *did* before the correct colour is obtained.

DID YOU KNOW?

Fabrics have different thicknesses depending on the weight of threads or yarns. It is measured in terms of *deniers*. The word *denier* comes from the French and refers to an old coin. The weight of one denier was said to equal a small amount of thread or yarn. In fact, the sheerness (lighter colour) or opaqueness (darker colour) of stockings is described as 10 den, 20 den, 30 den, 40 den, etc. Microfibres are less than 1 den.

AUDIO
8

7   **Listen to the promotional information from FabriTex's YouTube channel about its fabric production services. Put the services in the order they are mentioned.**

fabric testing _____   dyeing _____   finishing _____
embellishment _____   providing expert advice _____

8   **Listen again. Mark the sentences True (✔) or False (✗).**

1   FabriTex offers a choice of plant or chemical dyes.   ☐
2   They test for colour fastness.   ☐
3   The colour fastness of indigo fabrics is guaranteed.   ☐
4   For white fabrics they use a chemical bleach.   ☐
5   They have a finishing process for strengthening fabrics like denim.   ☐
6   They do not offer fabric printing services.   ☐

9   **Match the written care instructions for the garments (a–e) to the care symbols (1–5). There may be more than one possible answer.**

1   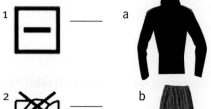 _____   a   This garment is treated using industrial dyeing processes that give it a 'lived in' look. Do not use solvents. Wash separately inside out at 30°C. Dry the garment inside out and do not expose to sunlight. Steam iron.

2   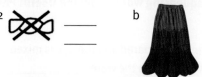 _____   b   Machine wash cold on gentle cycle with like colours. Only non-chlorine bleach when needed. Remove promptly from wash while still damp. Hold both ends, twist tightly and knot. Tumble dry low. Do not iron.

3   ◯ _____   c   Dry clean only. Do not machine or hand wash. Do not spin or twist. Low or steam iron only.

4   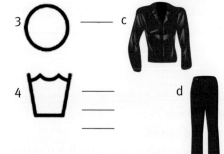 _____   d   The special finish of this pure cloth has original irregularities to bring out the natural aspects of the weaving and artisan dyeing process. A gradual change in colour is characteristic of this process. Wash separately with like colours at 30°C. Line dry, and iron on high.

5    _____   e   Wash by hand using mild detergent. Do not wring garment. Lay flat to dry and reshape. Do not dry clean.

USEFUL PHRASES: WRITING CARE INSTRUCTIONS			
Washing	**Drying**	**Ironing**	**Special Care**
Hand / Machine wash.	Tumble dry low / medium / high.	Iron on low / medium / high.	Do not wring.
Wash with light / dark colours / separately.	Line dry.	Steam iron.	Twist and knot.
Use mild detergent.	Lay flat to dry. Reshape.		Do not bleach
Dry clean only.	Dry the garment inside out.		

AUDIO
9

10 Listen to visitors at a trade textile show talking to suppliers. What textiles do they ask about?

1   a   cotton viscose
    b   cotton knit
2   a   animal yarn for vests, skirts, and sweaters
    b   synthetic yarn for sweaters
3   a   animal- and synthetic-based fabrics
    b   animal-based fabrics only

4   a   easy-care acrylics
    b   waterproof fabrics
5   a   fabrics that look like animal-based fabrics
    b   waterproof fabrics

11 Listen again. Complete the table with a tick (✔) or cross (✗).

Conversation	a Does the supplier have textiles the visitor is interested in?	b Do they look at fabric samples?
1		
2		
3		
4		
5		

USEFUL PHRASES: REQUESTS, RESPONSES AND OFFERS AT TRADE SHOWS

Offering
Can / Could I show you anything (in particular)?
Can / Could I help you find something?
Would you like to see (some samples /swatches)?

Requesting
Do you happen to have any (velvet)?
Could / Can I see some (test results)?
Could / Can I have / take a look (at some swatches)?
Are there any samples (I can see / look at)?
Is there any way to see how it (drapes)?

Responding to requests
Sure / Yes / Of course, we've got some samples / swatches (right) over here.
Yes, let me just get (some more information / our pricelist).
I'd have to check with ...

---

12 Match the sentence halves.

1   Would you like
2   Could I help you
3   Do you have
4   Could I take
5   Is there any way to see how
6   Let me

a   just get the test results.
b   find something?
c   a look at your price list?
d   to see some swatches?
e   any chiffon?
f   it looks in daylight?

OUTPUT

Fur: Real, fake, or nothing?

Since man first put on clothes people have worn fur, first and foremost because it's very warm. But over the centuries fur became exclusive and by the sixteenth century it was seen as a luxury textile. At that time, it was worn on the inside as a lining for coats, with only a little trim visible. In the early twentieth century, wearing fur on the outside of coats became fashionable. But more visibility meant more controversy and negative opinion. These days nothing in fashion divides opinions more strongly than fur.

What do the animal rights campaigners object to? Fur producers have often been criticized for bad treatment of animals, such as keeping animals in small cages and not giving them enough food and water. In response, fur producers say they run transparent operations and use clear labels to tell consumers exactly where their fur comes from.

The fight against fur has been led in recent years by PETA (People for the Ethical Treatment of Animals), the largest animal rights organization in the world. They have attracted attention for their often shocking campaigns, including a series of nude photographs of top models and celebrities under the headline 'I'd rather go naked than wear fur'. In the 1980s and 90s, fur sales fell dramatically and PETA's campaigns were a big factor in this. And with the improved development of fake furs, consumers found little reason for buying real fur.

The fur industry has hit back at animal rights campaigners, stating that real fur is much more environmentally friendly than fake fur. It believes that manufacturing fake fur involves dangerous chemicals, damaging the environment, and that real fur is natural and biodegradable. It has also said that younger women, inspired by celebrities, have begun to wear real fur again. Most major fashion houses support this renewal in fur by featuring it in a few pieces each autumn / winter collection.

It is impossible to predict whether the trend towards using fur in fashion will continue. Some say fake fur will overtake the real version. Others say fur is here to stay. What is certain is that wearing fur will always be a decision that divides people.

OVER TO YOU

- How do you feel about fur in fashion? Is it acceptable to wear fur, or should it be regulated or even banned?
- Will fake fur eventually replace real fur? Why, or why not?
- Do you agree with the anti-fur movement's shock campaigns? Why, or why not?

4 Garment construction

Label the equipment that pattern makers use (a–e) with the words from the box. Can you think of any other equipment?

> CAD software • cutting machine • pattern paper • plotter • sewing machine

a _____

c _____

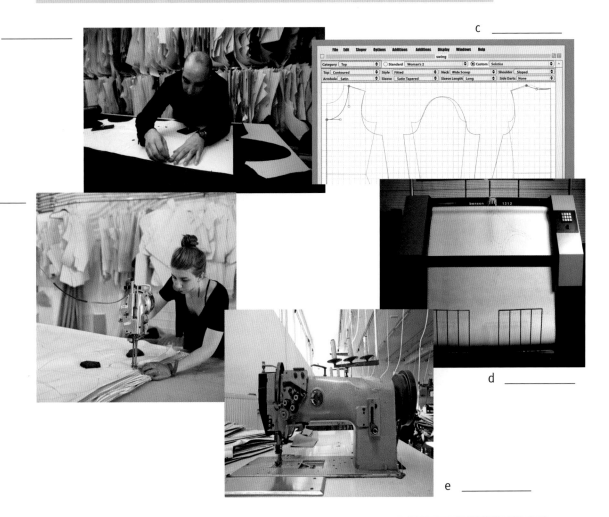

d _____

e _____

DID YOU KNOW?

Computer Aided Design often uses Pattern Design Systems (PDS), which are computer software programs that can digitally organize pattern pieces to be cost-effective. These programs can calculate the amount of fabric needed and its cost. They also make grading changes easier without wasting fabric.

1 **Match the stages in the pattern making process (a–i) with the pictures (1–9).**

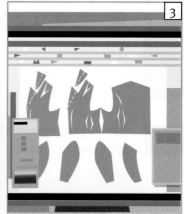

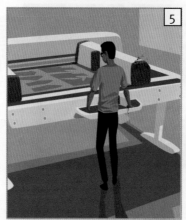
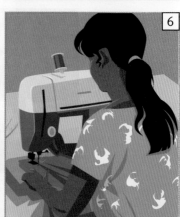

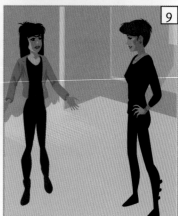

a cut a sample garment

b revise measurements

c sew a prototype

d develop specifications (specs)*

e lay out pattern pieces on CAD software

f approve the final pattern

g fit a garment on a model

h draft a preliminary pattern

i grade measurements for sizes

Specifications for measurements and pattern pieces usually is shortened to spec or specs. These are often listed on a specification sheet.

2   **Read the pattern maker's comments (1–6). Underline the correct alternative.**

	S cm / in	**M** cm / in	**L** cm / in	**XL** cm / in
Shoulder	56 / 14	38 / 15	38 / 15	39 / 15 ½
Around chest	81 / 32	86 / 34	91 / 36	97 / 38
Around waist	66 / 26	71 / 28	76 / 30	81 / 32
Around hips	86 / 34	91 / 36	97 / 38	102 / 40
Sleeve	79 / 31	82 / 32	84 / 33	86 ½ / 35

1   We need to *revise* / *sew* the sleeve by at least two centimetres for the medium size, so we'll have to take it in.
2   When we *laid out* / *developed* the spec sheet, we didn't include the extra small size.
3   Could we *draft* / *grade* all sizes to give an extra centimetre more around the waist for ease of comfort?
4   Remember to *cut* / *develop* the chest extra wide to allow for ease of movement.
5   Has the head pattern maker *approved* / *sewn* this spec sheet yet?
6   Let's wait until we *set* / *fit* it on the model before we make it any bigger.

3   **Label the parts of the body with the words from the box.**

> ankle • back • calf • chest (bust) • décolleté • elbow • hip • knee
> • lower arm (forearm) • mid-thigh • neck • shoulder • upper arm • waist • wrist

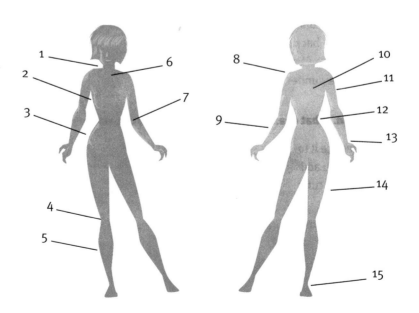

4   **Match the pattern pieces for a jacket with the words from the box.**

> back bodice • collar • cuff • front bodice • lapel • top pocket
> • top sleeve • under sleeve • yoke

1 _____   2 _____   3 _____   4 _____

9 _____

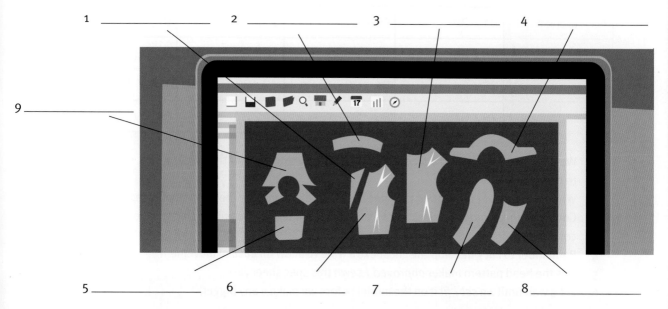

5 _____   6 _____   7 _____   8 _____

5   **Match the pattern pieces in exercise 4 to the parts of the body in exercise 3. There may be more than one possible answer.**

AUDIO
10

6   **Listen to five conversations about garment patterns. Which pattern pieces are mentioned? Choose the correct alternative.**

1   collar / cuff
2   top pocket / under pocket
3   back yoke / back bodice
4   under sleeve / lining
5   top sleeve / under sleeve

7   **Listen again. What changes are discussed for each pattern piece?**

1   cuff: reduce it to _____.
2   top pocket: add _____.
3   back yoke: cut it _____.
4   lining: sew it   _____.
5   top sleeve: let it _____.

DID YOU KNOW?

Different countries use different measurement systems for fabric amounts. The US, Canada, and Mexico use yards and inches, while most other countries use metres and centimetres. 1 yard = 0.9144 metres, and 1 inch = 2.54 centimetres.

USEFUL PHRASES

Discussing specifications
Are we supposed to ...?
Do you think we need to...?
Was there anything (you) wanted to change?
What does the spec sheet say?
This needs to be (cut horizontally).
We need to / We'll have to (add another pocket).
Look at (how the yoke cuts).
Let's see (how the fabric works).

Adjusting measurements
take (the leg) up (by 2cm) = make shorter
let (the hem) down = make longer
take (the waist) in = make narrower
let (the sleeve) out = make wider
allow for ease of comfort
take __ cm off
add another __ cm (around the shoulders)
centimetres, metres / inches, yards

8 **Complete the pattern makers' conversations using the words from the box.**

add • allow • let down • let out • take in • take off

1 A The jacket waist was a bit tight on the fit model, so we'll have to _____ it _____ a bit.
  B How much do you think we need to _____?
  A ¾ cm will probably be enough.

2 A The specification sheet for the women's blouse only gives the measurements for size 10. Are we supposed to grade a size 8 as well?
  B Yes. We need to _____ it _____ by ⅓ cm around the waist and shoulders for the smaller size.

3 A How many centimetres do you think we need to _____ for ease of comfort around the shoulders?
  B I would say just ½ cm.

4 A Look how far the sleeve falls on this shirt – it's too long. Let's _____ ½ cm so it falls exactly at the wrist.
  B OK. Also, the lower shirt hem needs to fall at the hip, not at the waist, so we'll need to _____ it _____ by 3 cm.

9 **Label the pictures of typical cuts and silhouettes with the correct words below. Which ones are fitted or loose fitted?**

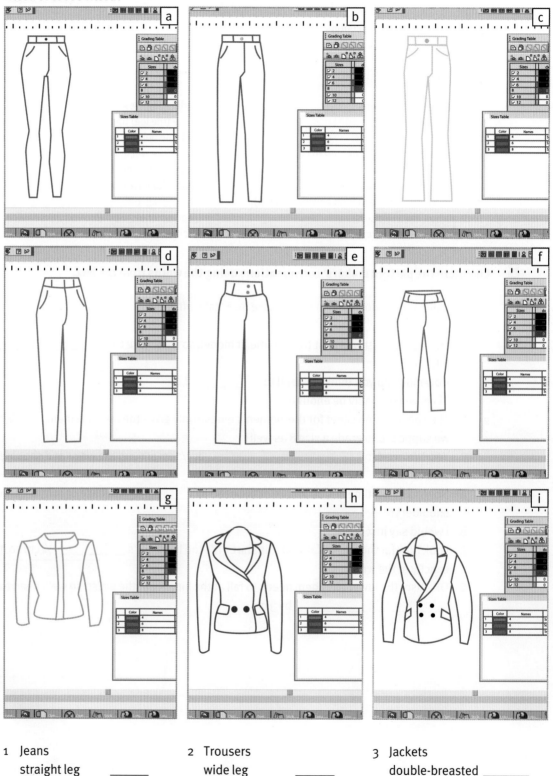

1	Jeans		2	Trousers		3	Jackets	
	straight leg	_____		wide leg	_____		double-breasted	_____
	boot cut	_____		tapered	_____		cinched waist	_____
	skinny	_____		cropped	_____		cropped	_____

AUDIO
11

10 **Listen to the designer and pattern maker at Fast Wear discussing their autumn / winter line. Which cuts and silhouettes do they mention?**

1 jeans _____

2 trousers _____

3 jackets _____

4 shirts _____

11 **Listen again. Correct the wrong information in bold.**

1 They're **confident** wide leg trousers would sell well.

2 The double-breasted jacket is **absolutely perfect** for the casual line.

3 The drafts for the fitted shirts will make the pattern 3cm **larger**.

12 **Look at the CAD garment pattern for a woman's blouse. Match the words with the definitions. Then label the images.**

> grading points • seam allowance • drill hole • right-angle • scale • notch

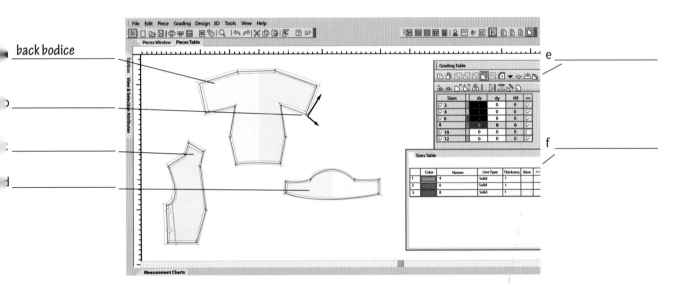

1 _____ a mark that indicates where design details (e.g. pockets, tucks, pleats, button holes) should be placed.

2 _____ a mark that is used to show where two pieces of fabric will be sewn together on a garment.

3 _____ the area between the edge of the fabric and the stitching line.

4 _____ places on a pattern where you want the size to increase or decrease.

5 _____ two lines set at 90 degrees from each other.

6 _____ a system for grading a pattern in different sizes.

Does one size really fit all?

Have you ever gone into one store and tried something on in your size, only to go to another store and find out that the same size is too small? Frustrating, isn't it? It seems that clothing manufacturers grade sizes according to separate systems.

It's important for clothing manufacturers to keep in mind their target market. But for a global brand, that market can vary enormously depending on the country where the clothing is being sold.

How does it fit? Let us count the ways
Clothing companies include style fits for jeans like 'tapered fit', 'boot cut' or 'low waist' to guide shoppers. Some clothing is labelled XS, S, M, L, and XL – that is, extra small, small, medium, large, and extra large – but an M in one country could be another country's L. Then there are the numbered coded systems. Germany has two different numbered systems for short and tall women. Great Britain often uses sizing codes ranging from 8–18, and the same numbers are also used in the US, but they are actually two sizes different. And in southern Europe, especially in Italy and Spain, a numbering system from 36 to 46 is used.

Help is on the way
Grading clothing sizes on real measurements is a good place to start. Mail order and catalogue companies are beginning to do this, and many give their customers detailed instructions on how to take their own body measurements. Customers can then compare these to the company's sizing chart. Some online retailers also offer a virtual 3D sizing model. There are different body types to choose from and customers can see different styles on a sizing avatar.

If a clothing manufacturer has a niche market, they may choose to produce garments that are tailored to a specific group of consumers. For example, Ferragamo is changing their shoe widths to accommodate Asian markets making them narrower. However, the European Committee for Standardization (Comité Européen de Normalisation) is working on developing sizing standards that can be applied internationally. Customers will need to know their body measurements in centimetres around the chest, waist, hips, arms and legs. Hopefully this will make for a significant improvement on the current shopping experience.

- What should pattern makers take into consideration when grading a line for sizes?
- Should there be one international sizing code? Why, or why not?
- Should the sizing systems currently used remain in place? Why, or why not?

5 Production

Match the stages in the factory production of garments (1–9) with the pictures (a–i).

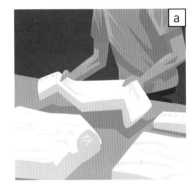

1	putting on hangtags	_____	4	bundling	_____	7	packaging	_____
2	laundering	_____	5	sewing or stitching	_____	8	putting on trim	_____
3	pressing	_____	6	folding	_____	9	label collars	_____

1 There were problems at each stage of the production of the white shirt in Starter. Complete the error comments for each stage using the words from the box.

> bundling • folded • hangtag • labelled • laundering • packaging • pressing • stitches • trim

1 There's a problem with the _____. There are only right sleeves. Where are the left ones?
2 There are skipped _____ on the collar resulting in two large gaps in the seam.
3 The black embroidered _____ doesn't follow the cuff line.
4 This shirt isn't _____ with the brand name on the inside collar.
5 The garment is not clean. It needs _____.
6 There are wrinkles on the shirt. It needs _____ so it looks ready to wear.
7 The _____ is wrong on this shirt; the size does not match the size on the inside label.
8 The shirt is _____ incorrectly. The right sleeve needs to show the cuff detail.
9 The _____ is missing for ten of the shirts. They were packed without plastic garment bags.

DID YOU KNOW?

There are several methods for assembling garments. In a single hand system, one person sews the entire garment. In a bundle system, a sewing operator does one or more tasks per garment and then sends the bundle to the next operator. Operators can also be cross-trained to work several machines and jobs in a modular system.

AUDIO
12

2 Listen to a quality assurance analyst and a factory floor supervisor discussing production problems with some trousers. Tick (✔) the problems they discuss.

1 The zip is too long. ☐
  The zip is too short. ☐
  The zip is broken. ☐
2 There's uneven sewing on the front pockets. ☐
  The quantity of front pockets is wrong. ☐
  The front pockets are sewn on top of each other. ☐
3 Too much fabric is turned in on the back pockets. ☐
  The back pockets are not turned in. ☐
  The back pockets are incorrectly sewn. ☐

4 The leg hem has not been stitched. ☐
  The two legs are different lengths. ☐
  There are holes in the fabric. ☐
5 The side seams are stitched with the wrong thread colour. ☐
  There are dropped stitches in the side seams. ☐
  There are not enough machine operators. ☐

USEFUL PHRASES

Explaining causes
It might be because + subject + verb
It might be because of + noun
The holes in the seams *are due to* dropped stitches.
Since the stitching is irregular, the hem is weak.
It's difficult to say, but …
It might / could / may / must be …

Explaining effects
The pockets were sewn differently so it looks like they are different sizes.
The hem is weak, which means (that) one trouser leg looks longer than the other.

3 Listen again. Why do they think the production problems happened? Take notes.

1 zip: It must be _____ .
2 front pockets: It might be _____ .
3 back pockets: It might be _____ .
4 leg hem: They may need to _____ .
5 side seams: It must be _____ .

4 Underline the correct alternative.

1 The hole is too small *since / so* the button doesn't fit.
2 The jacket lining has dropped stitches *because / which means* it might come undone.
3 This skirt zip is sewn wrong *because / so* it was not specified on the line sheet instructions.
4 I'm not sure why there's irregular sewing on the jacket but it *might / must* be the new machine operators.
5 The irregular sewing on the hem is *so / due to* poor staff training.
6 The shirt neckline looks strange *maybe / because* they used the wrong colour thread.
7 The stitching is irregular *so / because of* the pinstripes don't match up.
8 The side zip on the skirt doesn't work *since / due to* it's broken.
9 There *must be / means* a problem with the packaging as 30% of the shirts are folded wrong.
10 We'll have to sew the pockets again *because / because of* the pocket edges are unturned.

5 Label the pictures with the methods of packing.

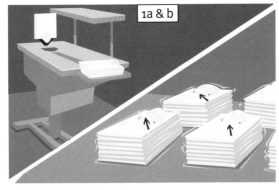
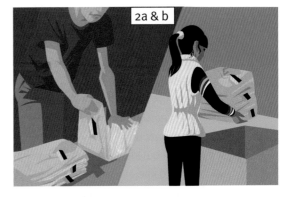

in plastic garment bags   machine-folded   in cardboard boxes
hand-folded   on standard hangers   in floor-length plastic
in rayon garment bags   on fabric hangers   garment bags

6   Match the comments about extra packing options to the pictures in exercise 5.

1   Retailers often ask our packing and dispatch division for cardboard, tissue paper and straight pins. This is so the garments don't wrinkle while in transit.
Picture _____

2   We commonly use full-length garment bags, which then go on an overhead conveyor that leads directly into a conveyor on the delivery truck. Sometimes the garments need extra protection so we put them on special cloth hangers.
Pictures _____ and _____

3   Sometimes retailers ask us to include hangtags so the garments are FRM, or floor-ready merchandise. Very often we package garments to lay flat in boxes.
Picture _____

7   Complete the retailers' descriptions of packing preferences with the words from the box.

> cardboard • folded • garment bags • hangers • hand • hangtags • hangers
> • overhead conveyor • rayon • straight pins • tissue paper

1   We are a high street department store and prefer that our evening dresses arrive clean. That means they must be packed in long _____ made of _____ instead of plastic. Then they must be put on an _____ which places them directly onto the truck.

2   As a menswear retailer we sell a lot of shirts. It's important that they are _____, either by machine or by _____. To keep the collars and sleeves in place we also request _____ _____.

3   We save a lot of time putting our garments out on the sales floor because they arrive already on their _____.

4   The silk shirts that our brand is famous for are very delicate, so we ask for a layer of _____ between the garments to protect them from rubbing against each other in transit from the factory to the store.

5   When our shirts go through the folding process, we require a piece of _____ between the fold to keep their shape. Since they go directly into plastic garment bags, we also ask that the _____ are already in place. Customers can clearly see the size and price when they're in FRM form.

AUDIO
13

8   Listen to members of the packaging and dispatch team at Clothes4All discussing their client's packaging preferences. Complete the table below.

Garment	Folded?	Tagged?	Bagged?	Boxed?
Men's shirts	_____ ¹	No	Yes, in separate plastic bags	Yes, _____ ² per box
Jeans	Yes, hand-folded	_____ ³	No	Yes, _____ ⁴ per box
Dresses	_____ ⁵	Yes	_____ ⁶	No

9 Listen again. What extra specifications does the packaging team report for each garment? Cross out the one request *not* mentioned.

a **Men's shirts:** cardboard, straight pins, tissue paper
b **Jeans:** on hangers, tissue paper, individual plastic bags
c **Women's dresses:** FRM form, tagless labels, fabric hangers

USEFUL PHRASES: REPORTING INFORMATION	
Asking what others said	**Reporting what others said**
Do you know what they want /wanted to do about +gerund	They said / told me (that) they want /wanted ...
	(Well,) they told me they'd prefer ...
Did they say whether/if they preferred ...?	They told me to make sure that ...
Do you know what kind of ... they'd like?	They (also) want us to ...
	They wanted to know if / whether we could ...

10 A colleague spoke to a retail customer about their packaging preferences for these garments. Write questions to ask your colleague using the Useful Phrases and the information below.

	Garment	Preferences
1	Skirts	On hangers?
2	Shirts	Folded with cardboard?
3	Trousers	Individual bags or 5 per bag?
4	Dresses	Plastic garment bags or rayon?
5	Coats	Machine or hand folded?

1 _____ ?
2 _____ ?
3 _____ ?
4 _____ ?
5 _____ ?

11 You spoke to a retail customer about their packaging preferences for these garments. Tell your colleague what the customer said using the Useful Phrases and the information below.

1 Dresses – individual garment bags, plastic hangers

_____

2 Coats – machine fold, individual rayon bags, hangtags

_____

3 Sweaters – hand fold, two per bag, 30 per box

_____

4 Jeans – machine fold, tagless label, 40 per box

_____

5 T-shirts – hand fold, hangtags, 100 per box

_____

Company Profile:

UNIQLO and its Takumi Team

UNIQLO is Japan's biggest and most popular clothing retailer. They also have an international network which extends across Asia, the United States and Europe through nearly 170 stores. They work with over 100 factories to dispatch their casual mix-and-match garments to their stores worldwide.

The strength of the UNIQLO brand lies in its particular quality assurance system. One reason why the Japanese retailer has been successful is because it demands high standards of garment production, thanks to the collaboration of their 'Takumi team'.

Artisans in a modern clothing company

Would you hire someone in their 50s or 60s to work for you? UNIQLO did and it has helped them stand out in the crowded ready-to-wear market. The 16 Takumi masters each have a minimum of 20 years' experience and expertise in sewing, dyeing or textiles. The Takumi team is both modern and traditional, reflecting the import Japanese custom of honouring tradition. Profiles of the Takumi masters feature in editions of the UNIQLO magazine, also known as *UNIQLO Paper*, distributed to customers in the stores. In this way, the company gets the message out to its customers about the high quality work that goes into the garments, and customers can see who is behind the scenes.

Educating new staff

The Takumi are responsible for passing on their knowledge to UNIQLO's production facilities in China. Each week they are present at review meetings to offer suggestions on improving sewing, or other aspects of production. For example, when design details prove unexpectedly challenging, the Takumi team will identify the problem and work with factories to identify strategies to overcome it.

A winning formula?

Can UNIQLO beat other large-scale retailers based on the Takumi alone? With so many different customers, the answer may be 'no'. But the customer is at the centre of UNIQLO's business approach, not just garment production. People entering the store are greeted immediately and made to feel like they are taken care of. More importantly, the company message is that customers decide how to style their own looks. The value UNIQLO places on communicating this message to its global customers may be the key to its success. From the Takumi masters making sure a shirt is sewn exactly as designed, to the in-store customer care, this unique clothing company has a lot to offer its customers.

OVER TO YOU

- How important are artisans in the clothing industry in your country?
- What benefits are there for clothing companies to gain in hiring older experts?
- Do you know of other clothing companies that follow traditional ways of making garments or accessories? Which ones? What do they do?

6 Promotion

Which marketing and advertising channels do fashion brands use to promote their products? Look at the map below and add any other ideas you have.

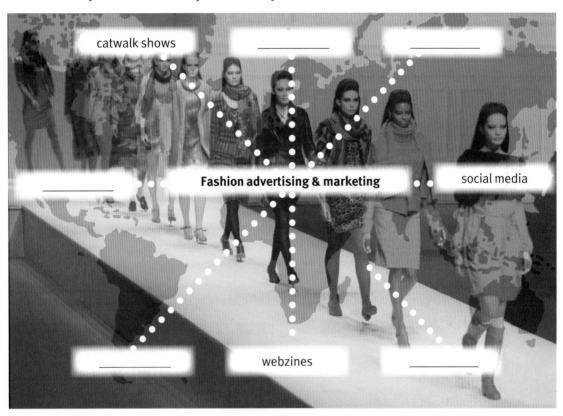

catwalk shows _____ _____

_____ **Fashion advertising & marketing** social media

_____ webzines _____

1 A marketing executive for a successful fashion brand is describing why they use different promotional channels. Match the words in Starter to the descriptions.

1 This forum lets us have a direct link with customers. They can leave comments or post pictures of their favourite pieces of clothing, accessories or shoes. We can also set up and manage competitions from here. _____

2 These seasonal events allow us to present our creative identity to the public. We present our collections and host events and parties. Journalists attend these events and write about them in magazines and newspapers, providing our brand with great publicity. _____

3 These online newsletters are a creative way to show customers how our designs work together in different contexts, at work, at parties, or on holiday at the beach. Customers can also read about designers, stylists and the whole creative process. _____

2 Complete the sentences with the words from the box.

> attract • create • endorses • launching • offering • promote
> • promotion • raise • priority • targeting

1 Our brand has decided to _____ our new jewellery line with a series of style workshops in key high street stores.

2 When a celebrity _____ our brand, he/she agrees to wear our clothing and the public associates his/her brand with ours.

3 We are _____ a younger demographic – twentysomethings – with our new ad campaign, by using photos of stylish models from that age group.

4 We are _____ our new perfume with a champagne reception on Friday evening at a high-street department store.

5 The band Planet X are allowing us to use their hit single in our perfume commercial. This will certainly help to _____ their fans.

6 Only for today, we are _____ a special 20% discount on purchases of two or more items.

7 Our range of diffusion lines, including perfume, accessories and housewares, helps _____ awareness of our brand in other markets.

8 We should make it a _____ to increase our online presence. It's really important to use social media effectively.

9 The new 3D TV ad campaign for our perfume will _____ a buzz when people see it. Everyone will be talking about it!

10 To follow up on its successful ad campaign, StyleN Fashions is planning a _____ using all our social media channels.

3 Match the expressions with *brand* to the definitions below. Do you know the brands in the pictures?

1 brand awareness ___
2 brand identity ___
3 brand loyalty ___
4 brand logo ___
5 brand name ___
6 brand recognition ___
7 own brand ___

a How much people know about or have heard of a label, or know which fashion house it is from.

b The word(s) used to refer to a product or range of products, like Onitsuka Tiger, Jil Sander or Diesel.

c When customers prefer to buy products from one brand.

d When someone can link the brand name, logo, stores, adverts, etc. with its products.

e When a retailer puts their name on the label of products, like Saks or Harrods.

f When a company gives a family of products the same brand name, logo, colour scheme, slogan, etc.

g A graphic design of a symbol representing a company name, often with a particular colour scheme.

BRITISH ENGLISH	AMERICAN ENGLISH
catwalk show	runway show
advertisement (also ad / advert)	TV commercial
homeware	housewares
lingerie	intimates
nightwear	sleepwear

4 **Label the pictures with the words from the box. What are the products in the pictures?**

accessories • fragrance • homeware • intimates and loungewear

1

_____

2

_____

3

_____

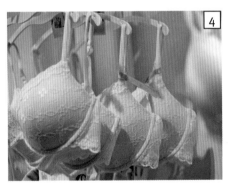

4

_____

5 **Can you add two more examples for each diffusion line?**

1 Homeware: towels, _____, _____.

2 Accessories: hats, _____, _____.

3 Fragrance: bath gel, _____, _____.

4 Intimates and loungewear: dressing gowns, _____, _____.

6 **Listen to brand managers talking about promoting their brands. Match each conversation with the product they are discussing.**

AUDIO
14

Conversation 1 _____
Conversation 2 _____
Conversation 3 _____
Conversation 4 _____

a homeware
b handbags
c intimates
d perfume

7 **Listen again. Which promotion methods are they using? Cross out the method they do *not* discuss.**

1 bus advertisements, a promotional discount, a webzine
2 a product launch at a museum, a TV interview, a photo gallery for their website
3 celebrity endorsement, online ads, in-store demonstrations
4 a flash mob, a behind-the-scenes video, a viral campaign

USEFUL PHRASES

Explaining objectives
The idea is (that) ...
The idea (here) is to ...
The objective / goal / purpose is to ...
The (launch) should be ..., so ...

Achieving objectives
For this to be effective, ...
To do that, ...
Another thing to consider is ...
In addition, we can /could ...
It's also important to ...

Prioritizing objectives
Our top / first priority is ...
First and foremost, ...
Above all, ...
Let's focus on the big picture for now.
Maybe this is less important, but ...
Maybe ... isn't as important.

---

8 **Complete the extracts from exercise 6 with two words. Listen and check your answers. Use the Useful Phrases box to help you.**

1 The _____ _____ that, as an accessory, we'll always be by your side, like a trusted friend.
2 Maybe this is _____ _____, but a website can offer a 'view inside' option.
3 This launch _____ _____ a memorable event, especially since we're doing it at the modern art museum.
4 Another thing _____ _____ is getting coverage in the fashion press.
5 First and foremost, the _____ _____ to get the customer to make a connection between her role as a TV mother and our crockery line.
6 The idea here _____ _____ increase brand awareness among 18- to 25-year-olds.
7 OK, although to _____ _____, we'd need a video editor.
8 Maybe the viral aspect _____ _____ important, but I like the behind-the-scenes idea.

DID YOU KNOW?

The first flash mob was created by magazine editor Bill Wasik. They started out as a social experiment with people gathering at an agreed place and then doing something unexpected. Flash mobs have since been used by brands such as H&M and Diane Von Furstenberg as a way to advertise, promote and market their designs.

9 **Complete the conversations about marketing campaigns with the words from the box.**

> channels • competition • customers • discounts • endorsement
> • focus groups • target market • viral campaign

1 *A* Apparently a Hollywood actress has given her (a)_____ for our accessories line. Do you happen to know which one?

   B No, I don't know anything about who's going to be in the campaign.

   A I haven't heard either, but I think it should be someone who represents our (b)_____.

   B I agree. Most of our (c)_____ are in their twenties, so anyone we feature in the advertisements needs to be someone they identify with.

2 *A* We've got some good marketing ideas for the new TrueBlue Jeans line from our recent (a)_____ . One of the participants suggested that we try to get a (b)_____ going on the internet.

   B OK, but it means we've got to have really high quality content on our website and social media pages, or people won't be interested.

   A You're right. We're also planning an online (c)_____ where everyone who posts a picture of themselves in TrueBlue Jeans gets entered to win a free pair.

3 *A* The store is planning on offering special (a)_____ to attract as many people as possible to shop with us over the holiday season.

   B So, what media (b)_____ are we going to use to get the word out?

   A We're running print ads in the major fashion magazines, and updating our website and social media channels, too.

10 **Susan Chiu is the director of Communications Direct, a public relations agency. Listen as she discusses with her assistants, Tomas and Rachel, how to promote a new brand, LeeAnn Designs, during fashion week. What promotional channels do they discuss?**

1 _____

2 _____

3 _____

11 **Listen again. Match the suggestions (1–6) with the responses (a–f).**

1 What about someone from the music or film world?
2 Better yet, why not get several cool young musicians and actors involved?
3 How about having a cocktail reception with the celebrities and inviting LeeAnn's business partners to attend, too?
4 I'd recommend including some loyal customers and influential journalists on the guest list.
5 Have we thought about organizing a flash mob?
6 How about doing it in a popular shopping street?

a That's a great idea. I'll get in touch with LeeAnn Designs and see who's on their contact list.
b That sounds great, but I'll have to check with the police first.
c That could become a pretty long list of names.
d Well, that might work, but we've never put one together before.
e I like that idea. How about a singer in a rock band?
f Good suggestion. I like it.

USEFUL PHRASES

Making suggestions
If + I could …
If I could make a suggestion …

+ –ing + noun
I ('d) recommend / suggest …
What / How about …?
Have you thought about …?

+ verb
Why don't (you) …?
Better yet, why not …?
Let's …

Responding to suggestions
Positive response
(That) Sounds good / great.
(That's a) Good / great idea.
Thanks for the suggestion.

Negative response
Well, that might work, but …
I'm afraid I'm not very keen on that idea.
I'm sorry, but I don't think that will work.

---

12 **Make suggestions for promotional ideas using different expressions from the Useful Phrases box, and the ideas below.**

1 use social media
2 include radio as well
3 ask a celebrity to sing at the party
4 everyone wear their favourite TrueBlue jeans at the event
5 journalists can tweet or blog about the event
6 have two flash mobs which meet up

WRITING PRESS RELEASES

Audience: Press releases go out to news agencies, so write with this audience in mind. Ask yourself why journalists would be interested in reading about a person, product, service or event. Why is it newsworthy?

Title: Use active verbs (e.g. announce, present, distribute, endorse) in a present tense. Leave out articles like *a*, *an*, *the*: 'Sylista announces historic guest designer collaboration with Urika Wantabe'.

Content: Explain essential information: Who? What? Where? When? Why? Use your company's name and the names of major participants and avoid personal pronouns (he, they, it, etc.). You may even include a quote from someone important. Keep the tone formal.

Ending it: Write an effective conclusion. Leave your readers with a memorable idea. Always include your contact information so journalists can ask for further information, if necessary. Finish with ENDS or – # # # –.

Read it before sending: Always read your press release before sending it. Look for common errors like missing subjects and verbs, punctuation, wrong –*ing*, –*ed* or verb participle (*They're interested* [*interesting*] *jeans*; *We have been wear* [*wearing*] *them a lot*); sentences that are too short (*It's a winner!*) or too long (*We're writing to let all stores nationwide and around the world know about our new, wonderfully smelling perfume that includes incredibly delicious scents such as cedar, rose, and musk, which were all found and created in our lab during the spring months last season*).

13 **Complete the press release about new perfume for U-Nique Fragrances by underlining the best alternative.**

FOR IMMEDIATE RELEASE
Paris, July 15, 20—

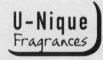

WE'VE LAUNCHED / U-NIQUE LAUNCHES[1] IT'S NEW FRAGRANCE: ***FLORAL-EVER***

U-Nique announces a new fragrance for summer. Open a bottle of Floral-Ever and a garden full of aromas will surround you. Floral-Ever has essences of cedar and jasmine blossoms.

Floral-Ever *will be distributed / will be distributing*[2] in stores at end of the month.

In addition to free samples in stores, there will be a *TV advertising campaign featuring the supermodel Prishka, and directed by Jim Furton / an advertisement*[3].

Known for his alternative movies, *he / Furton*[4] brings a surreal feel to the Floral-Ever image.

Pop band The Spin has agreed to lend a remix of their 1980s hit ***In the Garden***.

Marketing Now magazine explains the ad campaign team as 'a tornado of talent. Prepare to be blown away by the seductive imagery and sound'.

Everything is now ready for the launch. / Everything will be coming up roses with U-Nique's Floral-Ever new fragrance![5]

Please contact Jo McAllistar, U-Nique, Fragrance Division, 49-235-6793, jo.mcallistar@unique.com, www.unique.com/contacts

– #   #   # –

OUTPUT

The Fashion Short Film: Escapism at its best

Many people in the fashion industry believe that when you sell a brand, you have to sell a story. For some time now, the industry has turned to mini-movie ads to tell these stories about products. These 'fashion films', which can last from thirty seconds to four minutes, often bring together well-known celebrities and directors.

In the Chanel No. 5 story, for example, directed by Baz Luhrmann and starring Nicole Kidman, we see an incredibly famous star at a red carpet event. She seems to find the pressure of fame too much and 'escapes' from her limousine. Jumping into a taxi, she finds herself next to another passenger – an attractive young artist. With a smile, she exclaims, 'Drive!' The two then go to the artist's roof top terrace where he confesses he has no idea who she is. She explains she is a famous dancer. Throughout the film, we repeatedly see the Chanel logo, which reminds us that the story is selling perfume.

The film Bleu de Chanel also uses a story about a celebrity, but this time to sell men's fragrance in the commercial directed by Martin Scorsese. It begins with a male celebrity at a press conference, who is questioned about his infidelity. The film then shows us brief flashes of him and a mysterious woman, and of the same man trying to apologise to his companion or wife. Later, journalists put pressure on him to explain or apologise for his behaviour. He hesitates, and remembers his lover's face, which he then recognizes in the crowd. Suddenly, he says he will no longer behave as others expect. The final image is of the perfume bottle with the message, 'Be unexpected'.

The Gucci Guilty woman takes her role as a rebel seriously. In the Gucci Guilty mini-movie, we see her driving around a 3D city in a powerful Jaguar XK120 C-Type, leaving a trail of fire. Or is it a symbol of refusing to conform? She stops to breathe in the night air, and we see a flashback of a romantic encounter. Fully in control, the Gucci Guilty woman drives her own destiny. She leaves her love interest and drives off with mysterious music in the background. Depeche Mode's 1987 hit song 'Strangelove', covered by the group Friendly Fires, is the perfect soundtrack for this story of a woman who takes risks.

All three mini-movies are entertaining and have the look and feel of big-budget films. They are not just advertisements; they also offer a form of escape for viewers. Will the audience really get up to make a cup of tea or get a snack during a commercial break if the commercials themselves are so exciting to watch?

OVER TO YOU

- What other kinds of stories do fashion advertisements tell?
- Most perfume commercials are for women. Do you know of any others for men's fragrances, besides *Bleu de Chanel*?
- How important is music for TV ads? Why? Have you ever bought music because it was featured in a television ad?

7 Events

What is involved in planning a fashion show? Label the pictures with a fashion verb phrase.

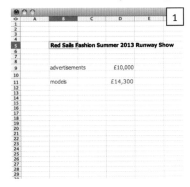

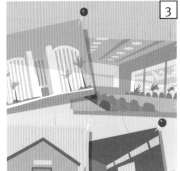

do a dress rehearsal   coordinate merchandise   choose a location
order advertisements   select models   make a budget
decide on a concept   find technical staff   send invitations

1 **Match the responsibilities (1–6) to the job titles (a–f).**

1 Fashion director   a finalizes models and lineup, sets choreography
2 Promotional coordinator   b chooses concepts, plans seating arrangement
3 Merchandise coordinator   c reviews merchandise, does fittings, pulls merchandise
4 Casting director   d sets up stage, tests lighting and audio
5 Stylist   e writes press releases, plans and runs advertising
6 Stage manager   f coordinates hair and make-up teams, chooses accessories

2 **Complete the extracts about fashion show planning with the words in the box.**

> pull the merchandise • print the programmes • decide on the seating arrangement
> • finalize their lineup • set up the stage • run the advertising • choose the concept

1

Casting Director: We've got most of the models selected, and just have to ¹_____,
which depends on which models are wearing which looks. Have you chosen the outfits yet?
Stylist: Well, I'm working with the merchandiser coordinator on that. But, we still have to decide
when to ²_____, and that means coordinating transportation and arranging a
delivery date for it. We have to be sure it arrives the day before the show.
Casting Director: And have you picked the accessories yet? It might help to know that the fashion
director and the designer have finally managed to ³_____. They've decided to do a water
and seaside theme for this spring / summer collection.

2

Stage Manager: We've got the floor plan and are going to ⁴_____ tomorrow.
I really like the Y-shape design and the raised seating!
Fashion Director: That's good to hear. I'm just waiting for the designer to ⁵_____.
We don't know who she wants to sit in the front row yet.
Stage Manager: Let me know when you find out and I'll set up the chairs with name cards on each one.

3

Fashion Director: How's the calendar for our promotional campaign for the show?
Promotional Coordinator: We're going to ⁶_____ and do the press release about four
weeks before the show, which gives people enough time to plan on coming to see it. Could you let me
know the order of the sets so we can ⁷_____? There should be one for every chair.
Fashion Director: Yes, I'll finalize that today. Don't forget I'll need to check the fact sheet about the
designer and the collection, too.
Promotional Coordinator: OK, I'll email that to you later.

> **DID YOU KNOW?**
>
> The first retailer to put music to a fashion show was Stanley Marcus in the 1920s. He used the Ted
> Weems band. Many shows today feature famous DJs and digital music, with live sets played both
> during the show and beforehand as the audience arrives. In New York City, Mia Moretti is a 27-year-old
> DJ who often includes very different music styles, such as Doris Day and The Rapture.

AUDIO
16

3 A fashion director, Gabrielle, is planning a show with the merchandise coordinator, Anita, and the stylist Frances. Listen and decide who will do these tasks. Write G, A, or F. There may be more than one person for each task.

Task		Person
1	Contact modelling agencies	
2	Tell the stage manager about the show concept	
3	Tell the promotional coordinator about the show concept	
4	Talk to the promotional coordinator about the budget	
5	Tell Alex about the e-invites	
6	Find a location	
7	Finalize the number of outfits	

4 Listen again and answer the questions.

1 What information do they need from the model agencies?
2 What is the deadline for telling the stage manager about the show concept?
3 What is Gabrielle going to talk to Alex about?
4 What was wrong with the venue Anita and Frances looked at?
5 Where do they want to find a location for the show?
6 When does Gabrielle want to meet the designer to discuss the lineup for the show?

USEFUL PHRASES

Delegating
Please + verb
(Can /could you) + verb
I'd like you to (handle that).
You'll have to + verb … by (the end of the week)
Be sure to + verb …
You're going to + verb …
Can you work together on that?
OK, do that and get back to me …
See if you can …

Responding
(Sure), I'd be happy to.
(Right), I'll do that (when) …
(Yes / OK) I will.
That sounds good.
I haven't done that that yet.
I still have to / need to …

---

5 Match the comments and responses.

1 Jan, I'd like you to handle the advertising.
2 Be sure to look at more than one possible venue.
3 See if you can send me the seating arrangement this week.
4 You'll have to finalize the model lineup by Friday.
5 Please talk to the casting director and get back to me.

a I will. I'll ask some art galleries if they rent out space for private events.
b Right, I'll contact all the agencies and let them know who we've chosen.
c Yes, I will. I'll call her this afternoon.
d I still have to ask the designer who goes in the front row.
e Sure, I'd be happy to. I'll coordinate with the promotional manager on all points.

6 Label the areas and people backstage at a fashion show with the words in the box.

> hair and make-up area • dressing area • floor covering • dresser • model
> • model sheet • lineup sheet • face scarf • clothing rack • mirror

1 _____
2 _____
3 _____
4 _____
5 _____

6 _____
7 _____
8 _____
9 _____
10 _____

SHANA

7 Choose the correct alternative.

1 Models go to the hair and make-up area ...
  a before getting dressed.
  b after getting dressed.

2 The dressers ...
  a help the models apply their make-up.
  b help the models get changed.

3 The model sheet ...
  a gives information about the model.
  b gives information about the catwalk order of the models.

4 The lineup sheet ...
  a gives information about the model.
  b gives information about the catwalk order of the models.

5 A clothing rack is ...
  a a place to hang clothes.
  b a place to iron or press clothes.

AUDIO
17

8 Listen to the five conversations. Identify the problem in each one.

Conversation	The assistant forgot to ...
1	
2	
3	
4	
5	

9 **Listen again. Complete the extracts from the conversations with one or two words.**

1 Well, not all of them filled out the contact information sheet, _____.

2 I'm terribly sorry. I _____responsibility for not telling them.

3 I hate _____ you this, but it looks like I didn't save today's file.

4 I'm so sorry. It was _____ to tell all the models about the floor covering.

5 I'm afraid _____ that one of the models went out on the catwalk out of turn.

USEFUL LANGUAGE		
Informing about problems	**Apologizing**	**Responding to apologies**
I'm afraid (to say / to tell you) that ... Unfortunately, ... I hate to tell you this but ...	I apologize for ... I apologize again. I'm (so / very / terribly) sorry I take full responsibility (for) .... It won't happen again.	I understand. Things can go wrong. OK. Let's see what we can do to remedy the situation. (Well), we'll manage ... You should (be in contact with them every day). OK, don't worry. / OK, but (from now on ...)

10 **Match the sentence halves.**

1 I'm afraid to say that there's   a   some of the models cancelled.

2 I take full responsibility   b   It won't happen again.

3 I'm very sorry.   c   but the new model forgot to use a face scarf.

4 I hate to tell you this,   d   a problem with the lineup order.

5 Unfortunately,   e   what we can do about cleaning the dress.

6 Let's see   f   for not reminding the models about the floor covering.

11 **Match the comments about fashion shows (a–d) to the pictures (1–4).**

a Glamour was the theme at the Diane von Furstenberg autumn / winter show. A gold leather belt added just the right amount of shine to accent the elegant silk black top and red skirt. Glam is back! Picture _____

b Bright, acid colours set a vibrant tone and accented the playful outfits. Picture _____

c The presence of red throughout the spring / summer collection lifts the mood and signals the arrival of warmer weather. Picture _____

d Sophisticated jewel tones closed the show: a treasure box of elegant dresses for any woman wanting to make a dazzling impression at a soireé. Picture _____

12 Read the blog entries. Match the phrases (1–10) to their synonyms (a–j). Write the letter of the synonym next to the phrases.

Colour Me With Stripes: The Kirwa Spring/Summer Catwalk Show.
By now, the Breton striped shirt, long sleeved or short, is a classic. In fact, I've packed four different versions in my suitcase for summer vacation. Stripes are great because they instantly (a) *lift an outfit* and bring a timeless air of holidays. For a relaxed, just-from-the-beach look, (b) *usher in* the start of summer with Breton stripes.

Gorgeous Accessories Glam Up Any Look: Fashion Week for Accessories.
There's nothing like gold and silver accessories to give your look an instant dash of glam. Local L.A. designer ZeeSuz has just put out a playful and deliciously (c) *fresh* line of costume jewellery. (d) *With a nod to* ancient Egypt, ZeeSuz's line is urban yet chic. There are bronze and gold bangles, scarab earrings, and Isis inspired wing necklaces. She has reworked the classic accessories to include Anubi belt buckles. With pieces like that, you can (e) *let the glam do the talking for you.*

Menswear Trend Report: Autumn.
At the Pitti Uomo show recently held in Florence, I can report there were a few unexpected turns. All styles and trends were visible on the catwalk. Expertly executed suits were (f) *paired with* print shirts. Edgy, kilt-inspired skirts in (g) *muted tones* presented an ambitious attempt to set the look for this autumn season.

Prints: What not to do. On the Street at Brazilian Fashion Week.
Fashion weeks bring out the best and the worst in people's wardrobes. "Prints (h) *with a twist*," you think as you plan your party outfit. You may believe you are being fashion forward, but think twice before you pair that striped shirt with prints or checks. It's a combination that simply does not (i) *work*. Use block colors of similar hues to pair, say, a black or cream-coloured top with prints. Or try a splash of neon colour, which will (j) *take it to the next level*.

1 matched or put together with _____
2 with an unexpected element _____
3 cheer, make brighter _____
4 recognizing the importance or influence of something _____
5 gentle (not bright) colours _____

6 have a positive or desired result _____
7 mark the beginning of something _____
8 communicate your glamorous style _____
9 improve something that is already successful _____
10 new, original _____

There are a lot of French words that are commonly used in fashion:
Clothes: *bluson, bikini, bustier, camisole, chemise, culotte, ensemble, lapel, lengiere, maillot*
People: *coterie, couturiere, femme fatale, femme, homme, modeliste*
Places: *atelier, boutique, maison, salon*
Adjectives: *blasé, beige, chic, décolleté, démodé, fashion faux pas, faux, haute couture, noir, nouveau,*
prêt-à-porter, trompe l'oeil
Other: *critique, crochet, cologne, denier, eau de parfum, eau de toilette, espadrille, je ne sais quoi,*
mannequin, motif, mystique, metier, niche, palette, parfum, silhouette, soirée, tulle

13 **Read an interview with a designer about his latest collection. Replace the words in bold with the French words.**

1	couturier _____	5	haute couture _____	9	prêt-à-porter _____
2	soirée _____	6	maison _____	10	atelier _____
3	chic _____	7	faux _____		
4	motif _____	8	palette _____		

I = Interviewer, D = Designer

I: Diego, as a (a) **high-end designer** you've had many successful collections. What inspired you this time to use a garden (b) **theme**?

D: Well, my (c) **fashion house** has a wonderful garden in the back, where I often go to think. And I also have an English style garden at my (d) **workshop**.

I: Are the gardens also the source of your (e) **colour range**?

D: Oh, yes, absolutely. Nature is the first place I go to for colour with any collection, be it (f) **luxury clothes** or (g) **ready to wear** lines.

I: I noticed you included (h) **fake** fur in this collection. Do you think you'll ever use real fur again?

D: To be honest, fur is a wonderful luxury. But we are going green, so we have to respect the environment, animals included. Personally, I think the fake version looks just as (i) **stylish** as the real version. Women could wear it during the day as part of the trim on a coat, or in the evening for a (j) **party**.

I: Diego, thank you so much for talking with us.

Give fashion descriptions using adjectives in groups of two or three: *The metallic details are **chic** and
modern. / Gold is an accent that is **glamorous, festive** and **fun**.*
Contrast two qualities: *strong but feminine, confident yet vulnerable, urban and still country.*

14 Complete the descriptions of the photos with the correct group of adjectives. There is one extra group you will *not* need.

a sensational, glamorous and modern
b young, relaxed and cool
c sophisticated, professional and business-like

1 The inspiration for my spring collection was free time. Imagine going out on a Friday or Saturday afternoon with friends and how carefree you'd feel. I tried to put that feeling into my designs and hope that the message is clear: these clothes are for a _____ look.

2 Everyone needs a bit of gold every now and then. My designs are for a night on the town, for special occasions, for when you want to be noticed, and especially for women who want to feel and look _____.

15 Match the adjectives to the pictures.

1 charming but practical
2 country yet urban
3 for a fun and easy-going look
4 young and elegant
5 edgy but still classic

Catwalk Diversity: Age, Race and Size

The catwalk has always been a place to showcase new trends in clothes *and* models. Ever since the age of the supermodel in the 1980s, models have become celebrities, and their social lives now fill the gossip magazines. More people than ever want a career in modelling. But are the doors to the profession really open to everyone? Is there diversity of models in the fashion industry?

Age

Although there are thousands of fashion lines aimed at the 30-plus crowd, the number of older models working at fashion weeks is very small. One Spanish designer, Juan Duyos, chose four veteran models in their 60s and 70s for the catwalk in Madrid's fashion week in the fall of 2010. That same year, the famous German model Veruschka, 71-years-old, walked down the runway for Giles Deacon at London's Fashion Week. But these are the exceptions to the large majority of young models on catwalks.

Race

Increasingly, we see more ethnically diverse models on the catwalk. A South Korean model, Kang Seung-hyun, was the first Asian to win the '*Ford Supermodel of the World*'. Other Asian supermodels include Du Jan from China, Hye-rim Park, who is Korean-American, and Eugenia Mandzhieva of Russian and Asian descent – they've all walked fashion shows for major brand names. However, some people suggest that the only way to increase catwalk diversity is to introduce positive discrimination, such as the demand for a minimum 20% quota of black models at the São Paulo Fashion Week.

Race diversity on the catwalk has been a hot issue for decades. Perhaps the defining moment was an event in November 1973 – 'the Battle of Versailles'. French and American designers competed with each other in a celebrity-packed fashion show. The French used elaborate sets and classical models to show off their creations, but it was the five American designers who stole the show, by using only African–American models on the runway. It caused a sensation, and the effects were felt across the entire fashion industry.

Size

One of the most controversial issues on the catwalk is size. One UK organization – All Walks Beyond the Catwalk – emphasizes size variety with their slogan 'Every body counts.' Their mission is to promote positive attitudes about body shape and size in fashion. The organization held a graduate forum on the size debate at fashion institutes in the UK in June 2010, and as a result, three colleges agreed that including a module on diversity in their curriculum was a good idea.

OVER TO YOU

- Have you seen age, race and size diversity on the catwalk? How many examples can you describe?
- How do you think catwalk diversity could positively affect people's image of beauty?
- Which groups do you believe are underrepresented on the catwalk?

8 Retail

STARTER

Label the tools visual merchandisers use to set up window and in-store displays.

mannequin • props • lighting • backdrop panels • merchandise
• glue gun • ladder • stapler • screwdriver • decal • tape measure

1 _____

2 _____

3 _____

4 _____

5 _____

6 _____

7 _____

8 _____

9 _____

10 _____

11 _____

1 **Match the display types to the pictures.**

1   in-store display _____   2   merchandise layout _____   3   window display _____

2 **Complete the descriptions of the displays in exercise 1 using the words in the box.**

> set up • install • angled • lit • displayed • dressed • stuck • hung

A
The merchandise layout has been _____ to allow customers to move around easily. The area is also well _____, so that customers can look at the clothes and see the colours properly.

B
In this display the visual merchandiser has _____ panels behind the merchandise to make it more eye-catching. The panels have been _____ from the ceiling. In addition, there are decals advertising a sales promotion, which have been _____ on the windows.

C
In this display the mannequins have been _____ with the merchandise, and accessories. The visual merchandiser has _____ the mannequins so that customers can see them from many directions. In this way the clothes are _____ to attract customers to a particular section of the store.

3 A visual merchandiser is explaining the layout for a store window to assistants. Match the comments to the images.

1   The sun prop hangs over the two mannequins.   ____
2   The mannequin goes under the lighting.   ____
3   Stick the decal in the lower left-hand corner of the window. ____
4   The dog prop sits in the forefront of the window.   ____
5   The umbrella display is next to the male mannequin.   ____
6   The other decal goes in the upper part of the window. ____

AUDIO
18

4 Listen to two visual merchandisers setting up a window display. Put the props in the order they mention them. The first one is done for you.

dog prop ____   decals ____
cloud props ____   accessories ____
blue spotlight ____   background panels ____
ladder __1__   screwdriver ____

5 **Match the sentence halves. Then listen again and check your answers.**

1	Could you dress the mannequins	a	me the screwdriver?
2	Do you need	b	about right.
3	Shall we	c	in the upper left-hand corner of the window.
4	Can you hand	d	a hand with the ladder?
5	How low	e	you stick the decals on the window.
6	How does	f	staple the two panels together?
7	That looks	g	work?
8	I'll do the lighting if	h	while I get the ladder?
9	Does the yellow spotlight	i	this look?
10	It goes	j	can the other cloud go?

USEFUL PHRASES: SETTING UP WINDOW DISPLAYS

Asking for and offering help
Could / Can / Would you hand / pass me …?
Could you help me?
Could you take a look?
Do you remember / know where …?

Do you need a hand with …?
Do you need help + verb + –ing
Shall we …. ?
Let's (move)…
Let me help you.
I'll …, if you …

Responding to requests for help
Sure. Here / There you go / are.
Here it is.
I'd be happy to.

Asking and talking about how something looks
How does this look?
How high / low can this go?
Does this look (ok / about right / fine)?
Does this (lighting) work?

(That) (It) looks (good / fine).
That looks about right.
Put it so it looks like …

DID YOU KNOW?

Window displays began in the nineteenth century, when factories began producing large glass windows for the first time. This gave rise to the storefront window being used as a way to advertise stores' merchandise. Today, many department stores have large budgets for creating very elaborate displays that often follow holiday or fairy tale themes. Celebrities and artists also contribute to window displays. Lady Gaga designed the winter holiday window for Barney's New York.

6 **Put the words in the correct order to make requests for help.**

1 stapler / Could / me / the / hand / you ?
2 look / this / take / you / Can / a / at ?
3 measure / pass / the / me / Would / tape / you ?
4 remember / you / where / the / Do / go / mannequins ?
5 hand / ladder / need / with / you / a / Do / the ?
6 first / install / we / Shall / panels / the ?
7 need/ moving/ Do / this / prop / help / you ?
8 go / low / can / How / lighting / this ?

7 Sahar Nazir, a buyer for a clothing retailer, is talking about her job. Read the paragraph and choose the best word or phrase to complete the definitions of the words in bold.

> As a buyer for a national chain of clothing stores, I need to make sure that we have a good **merchandise mix**[1] – our customers expect a variety of casual and classic clothing. I go to trade fairs regularly to meet with **wholesalers**[2], who can provide the range and quantities of products that we need. They will often offer a better deal for buying **high volumes**[3]. So, we might negotiate a **unit cost**[4] of £15 per item for orders up to 500 units, and then £12 per item for orders over 500. To avoid having lots of **unsold stock**[5] at the end of a season, I try to negotiate good rates on **buybacks**[6] with our suppliers. For example, I recently **placed an order**[7] with a supplier for 15,000 men's jackets on the basis that we could return up to 25% of them. Of course, there are occasions when we **overbuy**[8] and have merchandise that we can't sell at the full price. In these cases, we might **mark it down**[9] by anywhere from 10–70% depending on the month of the year.

1 Merchandise mix means …
   a a range of clothing of different styles.
   b promotional sales.

2 Wholesalers sell …
   a directly to the public.
   b to retailers.

3 When a retailer buys high volumes, they buy …
   a small quantities of stock.
   b large quantities of stock.

4 Unit cost means …
   a the price paid for one garment.
   b the price paid for one order.

5 Unsold stock means …
   a clothing or accessories that have not yet been offered for sale.
   b clothing or accessories that have been offered for sale but that customers have not bought.

6 Buybacks means …
   a merchandise that retailers can sell back to wholesalers or fashion labels for some of the original cost.
   b merchandise that wholesalers or fashion labels sell to retailers.

7 Place an order means …
   a enquire about the availability of stock.
   b make a formal commitment to buy a quantity of stock.

8 When a retailer overbuys, they …
   a order too much merchandise from the wholesaler.
   b don't order enough merchandise from the wholesaler.

9 When a retailer marks something down by 10%, they …
   a remove 10% of the stock from the store.
   b reduce the price by 10%.

8 Listen to a buyer for a department store negotiating with a wholesaler at a trade fair. Answer these questions.

1 Which garment is the buyer interested in?
2 Does the buyer place an order?
3 Do they reach a final agreement on delivery dates?

9 Who said these sentences: the buyer (B) or the wholesaler (W)? Listen again and check your answers.

1 I'd like to see what discounts you can offer us. _____
2 How many units are you thinking of ordering? _____
3 What would the cost price per unit be? _____
4 I'm not sure we can meet that cost. _____
5 For an order that size I can offer you a 10% discount. _____
6 I'll contact my supervisor and see what I can do. _____
7 That's the best we can do. _____
8 I think we have a deal. _____
9 Could you meet a shorter deadline? _____
10 I'm afraid my hands are tied on this one. _____

USEFUL PHRASES

Negotiating
If we …, can / could you …?
What kind of discount can / could you offer on …?
I'd like to see what discounts…

Proposing & offering conditions
I can … on condition that / provided that /
providing / as long as…
We can't … unless …
Can you meet us in the middle?
How does (20)% sound?
Could you offer us a discount of …?

Responding to proposals
That sounds fair (enough).
OK, we can manage that.
I can / can't agree to that.

Keeping a position
I'm afraid my hands are tied (on this one).
I can't go any lower.
That's the best I can do.

Delaying a direct answer
I'll see what I can do.
I'll have to think about it.
I'm not sure we can guarantee that.
I'd have to check with …
Is that your best offer?

Confirming agreements
It's a deal.
Let's shake on that.
We have a deal.

---

10 **Put the sentences in the correct order in this negotiation. The first one is done for you.**

Buyer

a   If we place an order of 10,000 units, could you offer us a discount? ____

b   Great. It's a deal then. ____

c   Well, we really like the V-neck and striped ones. ____

d   I'll have to think about it. How about 10% discount on 15,000 units? ____

e   I'm interested in your line of cotton T-shirts. _1_

Wholesaler

f   Let's see. For an order that size, I can give you a 5% discount. ____

g   That's great. Which styles are you looking for? ____

h   That sounds fair enough. ____

i   OK. Would you like to place an order today for those styles? ____

11 **Complete these negotiations. Use the Useful Phrases to help you.**

1   A: (a)_____offer us a discount on 300 units?

    B: I can only offer discounts for high volume orders of 500 units or more.

    A: Can you meet us in the middle?

    B: (b)_____. I'm sorry.

2   A: We can offer you a discount of 12% (a)_____you place an order for 1,000 units.

    B: (b)_____ my manager and then call you tomorrow.

3   A: So, we can't deliver the order in under three weeks (a) _____ you can pay 50% at the time of placing your order.

    B: Yes, (b)_____that.

TPUT

From High-Street to the Internet Highway: E-commerce

The expression 'go shopping' means something completely different today from what it meant 20 years ago. These days, you can go shopping from the comfort of your own home: online.

E-commerce is growing rapidly – it currently accounts for around 15% of all clothing sales in the USA. While bricks-and-mortar stores rush to catch up, e-retailers are taking advantage of the opportunities provided by the virtual marketplace. Some clothing retailers are turning to social media to build communities of customers who share similar tastes in fashion. In return for exclusive offers and access to restricted sales, customers are happy to share information about themselves, which retailers can use to build customer profiles and improve their marketing strategies.

Exclusively Yours, Online

One of the most successful fashion websites is Net-A-Porter, a luxury clothing retailer whose website is visited by over 2.5 million shoppers a month. Designed in the style of an editorial magazine, this inventive site offers a unique online shopping experience. This, combined with their style apps, offer customers a chance to personalise their purchases. Net-A-Porter's customers return again and again to buy from the site.

Other e-retailers, such as ASOS, have taken it a step further by using social media to bring in customers. On social network sites like Twitter and Facebook, as well as their own website, ASOS customers can express their inner fashionista by posting photos of themselves in their preferred outfits. They can also enter competitions, write blog entries, or sell second-hand clothing or their own new designs on ASOS' Marketplace. In 2011, ASOS attracted more followers on Twitter than any other retailer, and the rewards can be seen in their impressive sales figures.

Click, Pay, Sashay?

One of the key issues for online fashion retailers is how to get past the problem of customers not being able to try on garments to see how they fit, or touch them to get a sense of the fabric. Many e-retailers have tried to address this by including virtual models with 360° photos, video clips and detailed fitting guides. In addition, by offering online instant messaging or a freephone number for fitting advice, and efficient return policies, retailers can answer customers' concerns.

The Digital Future

Future trends in e-retailing include using social media even more and offering flash – or daily – deals through social networks. Many retailers are already offering virtual fitting rooms, mobile apps and interactive video technology. The online shopper can be sure that e-retailers will take advantage of every technological innovation to make the online shopping experience as easy and attractive as possible.

OVER TO YOU

- Do you buy clothing and accessories online? Why, or why not? Which online retail sites do you like best?
- What does online shopping offer to customers that in-store shopping doesn't?
- How have high street retailers used technology to respond to the challenge of the online market?

Test yourself!

Check how much fashion vocabulary you know.
Use the clues to complete the crossword puzzle.

Across

3 Sample strips of material. (8)
5 *"We made a loss in Year 1. Broke even in Years 2 and 3, and by Year 4 we were _____."* (10)
7 A spotty pattern. (5, 3)
8 Products are sold through a _____. (8)
11 The use of computer technology for design. (3)
13 The designer got a lot of _____ when the actress wore his dress on the red carpet. (9)
15 Scarves, hats, and bags. (11)
19 Someone buys in bulk and sells to retailers. (10)
20 An event where models show a range of clothing on a catwalk. (7, 4)
21 XTEILET: Another word for woven material. (7)
23 Term used to describe luxury, made to order clothing. (5, 7)
25 A reduction in the original price. (8)
26 The supermodel Kate Moss is managed by one. (5, 6)
28 A repeat of a design such as floral or tartan. (7)
29 Document announcing news to the media. (5, 7)
30 DERTN: A fashion or style of the moment. (5)

Down

1 The person who purchases fashion lines to sell in a store. (5)
2 Another word for inexpensive. (10)
4 GINLTROIA: the process of creating a bespoke or custom suit. (9)
6 "I got the _____ for the collection from travelling in Asia." (11)
9 Something expensive and hard to get. (6)
10 A group of people that a product is aimed at. (6, 6)
12 The autumn / winter _____ was well received. (10)
13 The _____ looked as good as the product inside. (9)
14 Stella McCartney is a famous _____ _____. (7, 8)
16 Trousers made of denim. (5)
17 Plastic model used to display clothes. (9)
18 A decoration on fabric made with thread. (10)
22 A fine wool used in luxury knitwear. (8)
24 To send off something. (8)
27 Change the colour of a fabric. (3)

Unit 1   Language test

1 **Choose the most suitable word or phrase to complete these sentences.**

1   As the PR manager, I'm responsible for the brand's public *trend /process /image*.
2   A *stylist / fashion designer /buyer* is in charge of negotiating prices with suppliers.
3   Working as a retail manager involves *manufacturing textiles /managing a team of staff / presenting designs at fashion shows*.
4   One of my key responsibilities as a textile factory manager is to *create a new look /oversee production /organize a product launch*.
5   I work as a *fashion journalist /designer/trend forecaster*. This means spending a lot of time doing interviews and editing them.

2 **Match the verbs with their alternatives.**

1	monitor	a	maintain
2	deal with	b	discuss
3	source	c	check
4	negotiate	d	find
5	involve	e	supervise
6	keep up with	f	include
7	manufacture	g	manage
8	oversee	h	make

3 **Put the following words in the correct order to describe the items of clothing.**

1   tartan green a jacket dark
2   pink a blouse pale long-sleeved
3   cardigan blue bright a floral
4   checked red and white shirt short-sleeved a
5   striped emerald knee-length skirt an green and black
6   dress polka dot yellow and white a

4 **Complete the sentences with the following prepositions. Each preposition is used only once.**

> into • of • at • on • with

1   What design details are you thinking _____ including?
2   We're looking _____ using a geometric print.
3   The team's working _____ the next promotional event.
4   Pinstripes are really popular _____ the moment.
5   We're promoting the new collection _____ an event in-store.

Unit 2   Language test

1   **Complete the text with past forms of the verbs below.**

Although western women (wear) trousers, or pants as they are also known, for outdoor work, it (is) only in the 1970s that they (become) acceptable in the workplace. It (is) Andre Corneques, a French designer who first (introduce) trousers as a fashion item in the 1960s. He (decorate) them with ribbons and precious stones and also (embroider) them. Then (come) trouser or pant suits, and in 1978 Gloria Vanderbilt (sell) her first pair of designer jeans.

2   **Order the following words to make past question forms about fashion firsts.**

1   jeans / began / 1874 / who / selling / in / blue?
2   Singer & Howe / what / invent / did?
3   who / supermodel / Quant / a / did / Mary / launch /as?
4   the / time / bikini / where /appear / the / did / first / for?
5   sale / nylon / when / stockings / on / go / did?
6   was / who / for / known / tailored / suits / her?
7   logo / what / designer / was / first / the?
8   ready-to-wear / first / which / created / lines / designer / the?

3   **Now match questions 1–8 with these answers (a–h):**

a   At a fashion show in Paris
b   Twiggy
c   An embroidered crocodile
d   Levi Strauss
e   Pierre Cardin
f   The sewing machine
g   In 1940
h   Coco Chanel

4   **Choose the most suitable adjective to complete these sentences.**

1   Many young people today have a *mixed / fitted* look: A tailored jacket with *ripped / padded* jeans and high-heeled shoes.
2   In 1955 Mary Quant created her own fashion pieces featuring skirts with *shortened / lengthened* hemlines and crocheted tops.
3   At the Spring fashion event many women were wearing trousers with *turned up / dropped cuffs* and flats.
4   In the 80s women wore *padded / pleated* jackets to look more powerful in the workplace.
5   Christian Dior's glamorous " New Look" featured *cinched / shortened* waists with full skirts.
6   During the 40s *pleated / printed* skirts became popular as they were considered very practical.

Unit 3 | Language test

1 Put the letters in order to make eight different types of fabric.

> OFCIHFN • RYOUCDOR • LRCAIYC • INLNE • AISNT
>
> KAMDSA • NXASDPE • RPSYOELTE

2 Put the fabric words into the grid around the central word.

						C						
						A						
						S						
						H						
						M						
						E						
						R						
						E						

3 Complete the text with passive forms of the verbs below.

Velvet _____ (make)[1] from many different kinds of fibres including silk, cotton, linen and wool. It _____ (weave)[2] on a special loom that weaves two pieces of velvet at the same time. Then a pile effect _____ (create)[3] and the fabric _____ (wind)[4] on separate rolls. After that it _____ (colour)[5] either _____ (dye)[6] or _____ (print)[7] and then _____ (finish)[8] More recently, synthetic velvets _____ (develop)[9] and also mixtures of synthetic and natural fibres such as viscose mixed with silk. Sometimes, a small percentage of spandex _____ (add) [10] to give stretch to the fabric.

4 Reorder the words to make offers and requests. Then match them to the responses (a–e).

1 help / I / particular / something /can / in / you / find?
2 can / any / are / samples / at / there / look / I?
3 list / at / take / your / I / a / could / price / look?
4 swatches / you / of / would / see / like / our / to / some?
5 I / statistics / some / could / see?

a Yes, let me just get it for you.
b Yes, that would be great, thanks.
c Of course, I've got some recent test results on my laptop.
d Yes sure, we've got some over here.
e Well, I'm looking for some synthetic yarn for sweaters.

Unit 4 Language test

1 **Match a verb to a suitable phrase in the pattern making process. There is more than one possible answer for each.**

1	cut	a	a garment on model
2	revise	b	a prototype
3	sew	c	measurements
4	develop	d	a sample garment
5	approve	e	specifications
6	fit	f	a final pattern

2 Put the letters in order to make seven different pattern pieces.

RLOLCA • EYKO • AEPLL • FFUC • LEVSEE • IOCBDE • CTEPKO

3 **Reorder the sentences to make a dialogue between a designer and a pattern maker.**

a Actually yes, we need to add 5cm to the waist to create a fuller skirt effect. ____

b That's great. Thank you. ____

c Don't worry, I've already ordered some more for you. ____

d Yes Tim, I have. Was there anything you wanted to change before we start sewing? ____

e Ok, I'll make changes to the spec sheet and start on the prototype right away. ____

f Hi Nicki, have you got the design specs for the Spring floral dress? ____

g Ok, but I'm not sure I'll have enough fabric. ____

4 1 Match the *verb phrases* with their definitions.

a	let (the hem) down	1	make narrower
b	take (the waist) in	2	make shorter
c	let (the leg) out	3	make longer
d	take (the sleeve) up	4	remove
e	take (the pocket) off	5	make wider

2 Choose a *verb phrase* to complete the sentences.

a We don't need an extra pocket. Let's ___ .

b The cuff is too tight on this sleeve. We need to ___ .

c The left trouser leg is 2cm longer than the right. We'll need to ___ .

d On the fit model the dress waist is a bit loose. We'll have to ___ .

Unit 5 Language test

1 Complete the stages in the factory production of garments using the words below.

> packaging • putting on hangtags • laundering • putting on trim
> • sewing or stitching • pressing

1 bundling
2 _____
3 _____
4 putting on labels
5 _____
6 _____
7 _____
8 folding
9 _____

2 Match the following sentence parts to give reasons for production problems.

1 I'm not certain but the irregular stitching
2 As all the zippers are broken
3 We can't complete the order on time,
4 The leg seams will have to be sewn again,
5 The sleeves have been stitched differently,

a because of dropped stitches.
b since there are not enough machine operators.
c so one looks shorter than the other.
d the batch must be faulty.
e could be the result of faulty machinery.

3 Match a word in box A to a word in box B to form packaging collocations.

A

> straight • garment • tissue • overhead • cardboard • hang • machine • cloth

B

> hangers • paper • tags • pins • bags • conveyer • box • packed

4 Complete the question and requests in A with a verb phrase in B.

	A	B
1	Do you know what they wanted to do about__?	we package
2	They asked if we__ the coats in rayon bags.	to put
3	They said they'd __ only two cardigans per bag.	folding
4	They also want us __the dresses in individual bags.	prefer
5	They told me to make sure that __the order as FRM.	could put

Unit 6   Language test

1   **Complete the gaps in the text with the correct form of the verbs in the box.**

> design • promote • attract • launch • offer • endorse • produce • create • target

David Beckham is one of the most famous sportsmen in the world. He is _____ [1] to both men and women and during his football career he has _____ [2] many different _____ [3], including watches, razors and clothes. In 2012 he _____ [4] his own line of underwear in partnership with the Swedish retailer H&M. _____ [5] by Beckham himself and Alasdair Willis, husband of _____ [6] Stella McCartney, this latest _____ [7] from brand Beckham is _____ [8] at men of all ages who like classic underwear. In the same year he was one of the faces who helped _____ [9] the London Olympics.

2   **Find the 'odd one out' in the sentences below.**

1 tableware	crockery	slippers	furniture	bed linens
2 scarves	sunglasses	wallets	bath gel	bags
3 nightdresses	gloves	pyjamas	loungewear	slippers
4 scented candles	hand lotion	towels	body lotion	powder

Match 1–4 above with its correct diffusion line below:

fragrance   homewares   accessories   intimates

3   **Put the words in order to complete the suggestions.**

1   you asking about thought have / journalists to tweet about the event?
2   about distributing how / free samples in the department stores?
3   why yet not organize better / an online competition to promote the brand?
4   we have don't why / two flash mobs meet up in the park?
5   recommend I'd inviting / a top model to the cocktail reception.

Now match the suggestions with the responses.
a   I'm not sure that will work. What if it rains?
b   That sounds good. People always like something for free.
c   Great! I'll get in touch with the leading fashion magazines straightaway.
d   I like that idea but what about inviting more than one?
e   Well, that could work but will we get a big enough response?

4   **Match the words in A and B to form collocations.**

A		B	
	flash		groups
	viral		endorsement
	focus		campaign
	celebrity		reception
	target		mob
	cocktail		market

Unit 7 Language test

1 Match a verb with a phrase to describe job responsibilities at fashion shows.

choose	the merchandise
set up	the press release
finalize	accessories
plan	the stage
pull	the models and lineup
write	the seating arrangements

2 Complete the sentences with the correct form of the information above and the appropriate job title from the box.

Fashion Director • Stylist • Promotional Coordinator • Stage Manager • Casting Director • Merchandise Coordinator.

1 As the _____ I'm responsible for the advertising and _____.
2 The _____ sets the choreography and _____.
3 Deciding on a concept and _____ are the responsibility of a _____.
4 The work of a _____ involves not only _____ but also testing the lighting and audio.
5 I do the fittings and review the merchandise, in my job as a _____.
6 A _____ is responsible for _____ and coordinating the hair and makeup team.

3 Put the words in italics in the correct order to complete the comments and responses.

1 *to sure contact be* the advertising agency
2 *that right do I'll* later this morning
3 *handle you like to I'd* the invitations
4 *need I check to* with the designer on that
5 *can if organize see you* a meeting this week
6 *done I yet haven't that.* I'll get it done by midday.

4 Match the French word with its English equivalent.

maison	workshop
motif	colour range
couturier	fashion house
prêt-à-porter	luxury clothes
palette	theme
haute couture	ready-to-wear
atelier	high-end designer

Unit 8   Language test

1 **Choose the most suitable verb and complete the display descriptions using the present perfect passive form where necessary.**

1   The merchandise layout *set up* / *install* to *allow* / *attract* customers to a particular part of the store.
2   Blue and yellow spotlights *light* / *hang* above the display to *make* / *see* it more eye-catching.
3   Behind the merchandise, panels have been *stick* / *install* and also *hang* / *set up* on the ceiling.
4   Mannequins *dress* / *display* with the merchandise and *stick* / *angle* so they can be seen from any direction.
5   Decals *hang* / *stick* on the store windows to *advertise* / *display* the sales promotion.

2 **Put the words in the correct order to make questions. There is one word you *don't* need.**

1   help me could for you?
2   this you look at take can a?
3   are props the know you where go?
4   the hand would to screwdriver me you?
5   the we decals to before do shall lighting doing the?
6   installing need do for panels you help the?

3 **Match the sentence halves to negotiate a discount in price.**

What kind of	can you give us a discount?
I'd like to see what	a discount of 15% on that?
If we order 200	discounts you can offer us.
I can offer	a discount providing you order more than 300 units.
For an order that size I	discount could you offer on the summer dress line?
Could you offer us	could give you a 5% discount.

4 **Reorganize the words to make short responses in negotiations.**

1   enough that fair sounds
2   I'll it about to have think
3   best can the that's do I
4   my I'm are tied hands afraid
5   on let's that shake
6   to sounds me good that

Answer key

UNIT 1

STARTER
1 a Creative director
2 c Pattern maker
3 b Machine operator
4 d PR manager
5 e Sales assistant

1
1 c   2 e   3 b   4 a   5 d

2
1 b   2 c   3 b   4 b   5 a

3
1 involves
2 supervising
3 is responsible for
4 networking
5 negotiating
6 Sourcing
7 come up with
8 monitor

4
1 d   2 b   3 a   4 c

5
1 drawing
2 identifying
3 sourcing
4 dyeing, analyzing
5 fitting
6 managing
7 promoting

a 4 & 5   b 1,2 & 3
c 6 & 7

6
Tops: blouse, cardigan, jacket, shirt
Bottoms: skirt, trousers
Whole body: coat, dress, suit
Accessories: gloves, hat, scarf

7
1 lapel
2 pocket
3 button
4 collar
5 buttonhole
6 embroidered motif
7 cuff
8 zip
9 hem
10 waistband
11 fly
12 seam

8
suit, collar, lapels, jackets, buttons, trousers, hem, waistband, seams, shirt, blouses, embroidered motifs, cuffs, pocket, coat

9
1 Yes
2 The design team is still working on the casual line
3 Leaving off the collar and lapels and reducing the number of buttons from four to three
4 a Embroidered motifs on the collars and cuffs
b Four front pockets and an oversized lapel
5 How much fabric they'll need per coat

10
Red: cranberry, burgundy
Yellow: mustard, sunflower
Green: emerald, teal
Blue: turquoise, teal, navy
Purple: burgundy, lilac
Pink: fuchsia, blush
Brown: beige, camel, chestnut

11
1 It's a dark grey pin-striped suit.
2 It's a navy and fuchsia geometric print dress.
3 It's a turquoise paisley top.
4 It's a multi-coloured floral skirt.
5 It's a mustard and black striped scarf.
6 It's a green and white checked shirt.
7 They're black and white polka dot shoes.
8 It's a beige and black animal print belt.
9 It's a red and brown tartan suit.

12
1 ✗ She's still doing research.
2 ✓
3 ✗ People are buying prints at the moment.
4 ✓
5 ✗ They're planning an in-store promotional event with models wearing the designs.

13
1 We're ready
2 figure out
3 are mixing, trend
4 We're, including
5 organizing

14
1 c   2 f   3 d   4 a   5 b   6 e   7 h   8 g

UNIT 2

STARTER
1 a   2 d   3 c   4 e   5 b   6 f

1
1 Sewing machines
2 Department stores
3 Designers and haute couture houses

4 Fashion shows
5 World expos and trade fairs
6 Licensing

2
1 Clothing became more affordable (cheaper)
2 Paris
3 It offered new ways to buy clothes, like mix and match pieces, and put on seasonal fashion shows
4 Music, dance and special lighting
5 Fashion weeks
6 They produced more affordable (cheaper) clothing lines (using the licensed designs)

3
1 began
2 arrived, used
3 organized
4 went
5 interrupted
6 did not put on (didn't put on)

4
1 used to be
2 used to be made
3 used to cost
4 (no change)
5 didn't use to wear
6 (no change)
7 (no change)
8 (no change)
9 (no change)
10 (no change)

5
1 got
2 appeared
3 (correct)
4 started
5 (correct)
6 (correct)
7 (correct)
8 (correct)

6
1 a   2 b   3 b   4 a   5 a

7
a 8   b 6   c 7   d 9   e 11   f 3   g 2   h 10
i 4   j 5   k 1

8
1 c (turned up)
2 a (fitted)
3 e (ripped)
4 b (dropped)
5 f (padded)
6 d (tie-dyed)

9
1 ✓   2 ✓   3 ✓   4 ✗   5 ✓   6 ✗   7 ✓

10
1 nearly disappeared
2 engraved
3 paid artists to make illustrations of his designs

4 wood blocks
5 less
6 illustration
7 all kinds of

11
1 engraving
2 hand-drawn illustrations
3 mixed-media illustrations
4 computer generated illustrations
5 silk screened

12
1 silk screened
2 engraving
3 hand-drawing
4 mixed-media illustrations
5 computer generated

13
1 engraved
2 mixed
3 generated
4 drawn
5 detailed

14
1 b   2 e   3 d   4 a   5 c

UNIT 3

page 23

STARTER
Suggested answers:
1 linen, satin, chiffon, lace
2 wool, corduroy, damask
3 chiffon, lace, satin, taffeta, damask

1
1 linen
2 chiffon
3 corduroy
4 wool
5 damask
6 satin
7 taffeta
8 lace

2
a 5   b 3   c 2   d 4   e 6   f 1

3
1 c (refining)
2 b (spinning)
3 f (weaving)
4 d (dyeing)
5 e (finishing)
6 a (embellishing)

4
1 sourced
2 removed
3 spun
4 woven

5 coloured
6 embellished

5
1 First / To begin with
2 When / Once
3 Before
4 Then / Next / After that
5 then / after that
6 Finally / In the last stage

6
1 ~~weaved~~ woven
2 ~~spinned~~ spun
3 ~~embellishing~~ embellished
4 ~~died~~ dyed
5 ~~did~~ done

7
1 dyeing
2 fabric testing
3 finishing
4 embellishment
5 providing expert advice

8
1 ✓ 2 ✓ 3 ✗ 4 ✓ 5 ✗ 6 ✗

9
1 e 2 c, e 3 c 4 a, b, d 5 a, c, d

10
1 b 2 a 3 a 4 b 5 a

11
1 a ✓ b ✓
2 a ✓ b ✗
3 a ✓ b ✓
4 a ✓ b ✓
5 a ✗ b ✗

12
1 d 2 b 3 e 4 c 5 f 6 a

UNIT 4

page 29

STARTER
a pattern paper
b cutting machine
c CAD software
d plotter
e sewing machine
Other equipment may include, but is not limited to:
tracing tools, rulers, scissors, awl (pointed tool for
making holes by hand)

1
1 h 2 d 3 e 4 i 5 a 6 c 7 g 8 b 9 f

2
1 revise
2 developed

3 grade
4 cut
5 approved
6 fit
S 67 / 27, **M** = 72 / 29,
L 77 / 31, **SL** = 82 / 33,
Sleeve: M = 80 / 30

3
1 neck 2 chest (bust) 3 hip 4 knee 5 calf
6 décolleté 7 elbow 8 shoulder
9 lower arm (forearm) 10 back 11 upper arm
12 waist 13 wrist 14 mid-thigh 15 ankle

4
1 lapel
2 cuff
3 back bodice
4 collar
5 top pocket
6 front bodice
7 top sleeve
8 under sleeve
9 yoke

5
1 lapel, chest, shoulders
2 cuff; wrist
3 top sleeve, upper and lower arm
4 under sleeve, upper and lower arm, underarm
5 collar, neck
6 back bodice, back
7 front bodice, chest
8 yoke; shoulders, back
9 top pocket, waist, chest

6
1 cuff
2 top pocket
3 back yoke
4 lining
5 top sleeve

7
1 5cm
2 another
3 horizontally
4 without the lining
5 out

8
1 let ... out, add
2 take ... in
3 allow
4 take off, let ... down

9
1 a skinny   b straight leg   c boot cut
2 d tapered   e wide leg   f cropped
3 g cropped   h cinched waist   i double breasted

10
1 boot cut
2 wide leg, tapered
3 double-breasted, cinched waist, cropped
4 loose fit, fitted

11
1 They are not sure that having two wide leg trouser types in the same collection is a good idea. They discuss including a tapered trouser, but do not make a final decision.
2 They won't include the double breasted jacket in the collection because it is too formal for the casual line.
3 They are going to take in the loose-fit shirt by 3 cm to make the fitted shirt pattern.

12
1 drill hole
2 notch
3 seam allowance
4 grading points
5 right angle
6 scale

a back bodice
b right angle
c front bodice
d collar
e grading table
f sizes table

UNIT 5

page 37

STARTER

1 g 2 e 3 f 4 a 5 b 6 h 7 i
8 c 9 d

1
1 bundling
2 stitches
3 trim
4 labelled
5 laundering
6 pressing
7 hangtag
8 folded
9 packaging

2
1 The zip is broken.
2 The front pockets are sewn on top of each other.
3 The back pockets are not turned in.
4 The two legs are different lengths.
5 There are dropped stitches in the side seams.

3
1 ... a faulty batch of zips.
2 ... due to the new machinery. The operators are still being trained on using the new machines, so they don't produce consistent results.
3 ... the new staff and their unfinished training.
4 ... check the stitching more frequently (hourly).
5 ... a mechanical problem.

4
1 so
2 which means
3 because
4 might
5 due to
6 because
7 so
8 since
9 must be
10 because

5
1 a machine-folded   b in plastic garment bags
2 a hand-folded   b in cardboard boxes
3 a on standard hangers b in rayon garment bags
4 a on fabric hangers   b in floor-length plastic garment bags

6
1 Pictures 1a and 1b
2 Pictures 4 a and 4 b
3 Picture 2 b

7
1 garment bags, rayon, overhead conveyor
2 folded, hand, straight pins
3 hangers
4 tissue paper
5 cardboard, hangtags

8
1 Yes, machine-folded
2 25
3 Yes
4 50
5 No
6 Yes, in rayon garment bags

9
1 tissue paper
2 on hangers
3 tagless labels

10
Suggested answers:
1 Did they say whether they wanted the skirts on hangers?
2 Do you know if they'd prefer the shirts folded with cardboard?
3 Do you know whether they preferred individual bags or 5 per bag?
4 Do you know what kind of garment bag they'd like?
5 Did they say if they'd prefer the coats machine- or hand-folded?

11
Suggested answers:
1 They said that they want the dresses in individual garment bags and on plastic hangers.
2 They also want us to machine-fold the coats and put them in individual rayon bags with hangtags on them.
3 They told me to make sure the sweaters are hand-folded, with two per bag and 30 per box.
4 They'd prefer us to hand-fold them, put on a tagless label, and pack them 40 per box.
5 They want us to hand fold the T-shirts, put hang-tags on them and pack them 100 per box.

UNIT 6

page 43

STARTER

Suggested answers: in-store events, pre-sales for preferred customers, twitter feeds, television interviews, celebrity endorsements, advertising campaigns (print and media), customer sweepstakes or competitions to win products, magazine editorials, apps for smart tablets

1
1 social media
2 catwalk shows
3 webzines

2
1 promote
2 endorses
3 targeting
4 launching
5 attract
6 offering
7 raise
8 priority
9 create
10 promotion

3
1 a   2 f   3 c   4 g   5 b   6 d   7 e

4
1 homeware (bed linen)
2 fragrance (perfume)
3 accessories (handbags)
4 intimates and loungeware (lingerie)

5
Suggested answers:
1 bed linen, crockery, furniture, tableware
2 gloves, scarves, bags, sunglasses, key chains, wallets
3 body / hand lotion, powder, scented candles
4 pyjamas, nightdresses, loungewear, lingerie

6
1 b   2 d   3 a   4 c

7
1 bus advertisements
2 a TV interview
3 online ads
4 a flash mob

8
1 idea is
2 less important
3 should be
4 to consider
5 goal is
6 is to
7 do that
8 isn't as

9
1 a endorsement
  b target market
  c customers
2 a focus groups
  b viral campaign
  c competition
3 a discounts
  b channels

10
1 celebrity endorsement (with young musicians or actors)
2 a cocktail reception (with celebrities and business partners)
3 a flash mob

11
1 e   2 f   3 a   4 c   5 d   6 b

12
Suggested answers:
1 Why don't we use social media?
2 How about including radio as well?
3 Let's ask a celebrity to sing at the party.
4 Better yet, why not ask everyone to wear their favorite TrueBlue jeans at the event?
5 Have you thought about asking journalists to tweet or blog about the event?
6 I'd suggest having two flash mobs which meet up.

13
1 U-NIQUE LAUNCHES
2 will be distributed
3 a TV advertisement campaign featuring the supermodel Prishka, and directed by Jim Furton
4 Furton
5 Everything will be coming up roses with U-Nique's Floral-Ever new fragrance!

UNIT 7

page 51

STARTER

1 make a budget, 2 decide on a concept, 3 choose a location, 4 find technical staff, 5 coordinate merchandise, 6 select models, 7 order advertisements, 8 send invitations, 9 do a dress rehearsal

1
1 b   2 e   3 c   4 a   5 f   6 d

2
1 finalize their lineup
2 pull the merchandise
3 choose the concept
4 set up the stage
5 decide on the seating arrangement
6 run the advertising
7 print the programmes

3
1 A   2 F   3 A   4 G   5 A   6 A & F   7 G & F

4
1 They need the agencies' daily rates
2 By the end of the week
3 The budget for advertisements and invitations
4 It was too small
5 Near the river
6 Next Tuesday afternoon

5
1 e   2 a   3 d   4 b   5 c

6
1 face towel 2 lineup sheet 3 dresser 4 model
5 model sheet 6 mirror 7 clothing rack 8 dressing
area 9 hair and make up area 10 floor covering
7
1 a   2 b   3 a   4 b   5 a

8
1 The assistant forgot to get all the models' contact
  information.
2 The assistant forgot to send the builders an
  updated floor plan.
3 The assistant forgot to save today's work file on her
  computer.
4 The assistant forgot to remind the model to stand
  on the floor covering while getting changed.
5 The assistant forgot to follow the lineup sheet.

9
1 unfortunately, 2 take full, 3 to tell, 4 my
responsibility, 5 to say

10
1 d   2 f   3 b   4 c   5 a   6 e

11
a : image 4,   b : image 2,   c : image 1,   d : image 3

12
1 f   2 h   3 a   4 d   5 g   6 i   7 b   8 e
9 j   10 c

13
1 a   2 j   3 i   4 b   5 f   6 c   7 h   8 e
9 g   10 d

14
1 b   2 a

15
a 1   b 5   c 4   d 3   e 2

UNIT 8

page 60

STARTER
1 lighting 2 backdrop panels 3 decal 4 props
5 glue gun 6 mannequin 7 merchandise 8 ladder
9 screwdriver 10 stapler 11 tape measure

1
1 1 c   2 a   3 b

2 A set up, lit
      B installed, hung, stuck
      C dressed, angled, displayed

3 1 d   2 f   3 b,   4 a   5 e   6 c

4
1 ladder   2 accessories   3 background panels
4 cloud props   5 screwdriver   6 dog prop
7 decals   8 blue spotlight

5
1 h   2 d   3 f   4 a   5 j   6 i   7 b   8 e
9 g   10 c

6
1 Could you hand me the stapler?
2 Can you take a look at this?
3 Would you pass me the tape measure?
4 Do you remember where the mannequins go?
5 Do you need a hand with the ladder?
6 Shall we install the panels first?
7 Do you need help moving this prop?
8 How low can this lighting go?

7
1 a   2 b   3 b   4 a   5 b   6 a   7 b   8 a   9 b

8
1 a brown linen skirt, 2 yes – 31 euros per unit for the
first 400 units, and then 32 euros per unit for any
orders above that, 3 no

9
1 B   2 W   3 B   4 B   5 W   6 W   7 W   8 B
9 B   10 W

10
1 e   2 g   3 c   4 i   5 a   6 f   7 d   8 h   9 b

11
1 a Would / Could / Can you, b I'm afraid my hands
are tied / I can't go any lower / That's the best I can
do 2 a on condition that / provided that / providing /
as long as, b I'd have to check with 3 a unless b let's
shake on

TEST YOURSELF

page 68

Across		Down	
3	swatches	1	buyer
5	profitable	2	affordable
7	polka dot	4	tailoring
8	retailer	6	inspiration
11	CAD	9	luxury
13	publicity	10	target market
15	accessories	12	collection
19	wholesaler	13	packaging
20	fashion show	14	fashion designer
21	textile	16	jeans
23	haute couture	17	mannequin
25	discount	18	embroidery
26	model agency	22	cashmere
28	pattern	24	dispatch
29	press release	27	dye
30	trend		

Test answer key

UNIT 1

page 70

1

1 image 2 buyer 3 managing a team of staff 4 oversee production 5 fashion journalist

2

monitor/check deal with/ manage source/find negotiate/discuss involve/include keep up with/ maintain manufacture/make oversee/supervise

3

1   a dark green tartan jacket
2   a pale pink long-sleeved blouse
3   a bright blue floral cardigan
4   a red and white checked short-sleeved shirt
5   an emerald green and black striped knee-length skirt
6   a yellow and white polka dot dress

4

1   What design details are you thinking *of* including?
2   We're looking *into* using a geometric print.
3   The team's working *on* the next promotional event.
4   Pinstripes are really popular *at* the moment.
5   We're promoting the new collection *with* an event in-store.

UNIT 2

page 71

1

wore, was, became, was, introduced, decorated, embroidered, came, sold

2

1   Who began selling blue jeans in 1874?
2   What did Singer & Howe invent?
3   Who did Mary Quant launch as a supermodel?
4   Where did the bikini appear for the first time?
5   When did nylon stockings go on sale?
6   Who was known for her tailored suits?
7   What was the first designer logo?
8   Which designer created the first ready to wear lines?

3

1 Levi Strauss 2 The sewing machine 3 Twiggy 4 At a fashion show in Paris 5 In 1940 6 Coco Chanel 7 An embroidered crocodile 8 Pierre Cardin

4

1 mixed 2 shortened 3 turned up 4 padded 5 cinched 6 pleated

UNIT 3

page 72

1

chiffon, corduroy, acrylic, linen, satin, damask, spandex, polyester

2

				a	C	r	y	l	i	c
			s	p	A	n	d	e	x	
					S	a	t	i	n	
				c	H	i	f	f	o	n
				d	a	M	a	s	k	
		p	o	l	y	E	s	t	e	r
c	o	r	d	u	R	o	y			
				l	i	n	E	n		

3

1 is made 2 is woven 3 is created 4 is wound 5 is coloured 6 dyed 7 printed 8 finished 9 have been developed 10 is added

4

1   Can I help you find something in particular?
2   Are there any samples I can look at?
3   Could I take a look at your price list?
4   Would you like to see some of our swatches?
5   Could I see some statistics?

1 e 2 d 3 a 4 b 5 c

UNIT 4

page 73

1

1 d 2 c 3 b 4 e 5 f 6 a

2

collar yoke lapel cuff sleeve bodice pocket

3

1 f 2 d 3 a 4 g 5 c 6 e

4

1 a3 b1 c5 d2 e4
2 a take it off b let it out c take it up d take it in

UNIT 5

page 74

1
2 sewing or stitching
3 putting on trim
5 laundering
6 pressing
7 putting on hangtags
9 packaging

2
1 e 2 d 3 b 4 a 5 c

3
straight pins / garment bags / tissue paper/ overhead conveyer / cardboard box / hang tags / machine packed / cloth hangers

4
1 Do you know what they wanted to do about *folding*?
2 They asked if we *could put* the coats in the rayon bags.
3 They said they'd *prefer* only two cardigans per bag.
4 They also want us *to put* the dress in individual bags.
5 They told me to make sure *we package* the order as FRM.

UNIT 6

page 75

1
1 attractive 2 endorsed 3 products 4 launched
5 created 6 designed 7 offering 8 targeted 9 promote

2
1 slippers 2 bath gel 3 gloves 4 towels
fragrance 4 homewares 1 accessories 2 intimates

3
1 Have you thought about asking
2 How about distributing
3 Better yet; why not organize
4 Why don't we have
5 I'd recommend inviting

1 e 2 b 3 c 4 a 5 d

4
Flash mob Viral campaign Focus groups Celebrity endorsement Target market Cocktail reception

UNIT 7

page 76

1
Choose accessories
Set up the stage
Finalize the models and lineup
Plan the seating arrangements
Pull the merchandise
Write the press release

2
1 PR manager / writing the press release.
2 casting director / selects the models and line up
3 fashion director / seating arrangements
4 stage manager / setting up the stage
5 merchandise manager / pull the merchandise
6 stylist / choosing the accessories

3
1 Be sure to contact
2 Right I'll do that
3 I'd like you to handle
4 I need to check
5 See if you can organize
6 I haven't done that yet

4
maison / fashion house
motif / theme
couturier / high-end designer
prêt-á-porter / ready to wear
palette / colour range
haute couture/ luxury
clothes atelier / workshop

UNIT 8

page 77

1
1 has been set up / attract
2 have been hung / make
3 installed / hung
4 have been dressed / angled
5 have been stuck / to advertise

2
1 Could you help me? *for*
2 Can you take a look? *at*
3 Do you know where the props go? *are*
4 Would you hand me the screwdriver? *to*
5 Shall we do the lighting before doing the decals? *to*
6 Do you need help installing the panels? *for*

3
What kind of discount could you offer on the summer dress line?
I'd like to see what discounts you can offer us.
If we order 200 can you give us a discount?
For an order that size I could give you a 5% discount.
Could you offer us a discount of 15% on that?

4
1 That *sounds* fair enough
2 I'll have to *think* about it
3 That's the *best* I can do
4 My hands are *tied* I'm afraid
5 Let's *shake* on that
6 That *sounds* good to me

Transcripts

UNIT 1, EXERCISE 1

1

My job involves crazy hours. You've got to be very flexible and personable because you're constantly working with people's public image. This can be especially challenging with celebrity clients, and I've had to work a lot on communicating clearly with them. I love it when we've put together a few looks and a client says, "Wow. I never would have thought about wearing it like that" or "I usually don't wear those colours, but they actually work well."

2

What's the best thing about my job? Well, I really like the fact that it's varied: from supervising my team and providing them with the support they need to do their jobs, to generating ideas for a new publicity campaign, or organizing an in-store product launch. I never get bored. I've even had to write speeches for our designers when they've received industry awards. The hours are long, but no two weeks are ever the same.

3

I need lots of different skills in my job. Basically, we are like fortune-tellers predicting what people will want to be wearing 18 to 24 months in advance. We need to be able to communicate our vision using hand-drawn or digital sketches. We also have to build good relationships with textile manufacturers, so that we can find the right fabrics for our designs. We are team leaders, supervising the production and the creation of prototypes. And, last but not least, we are showmen, presenting our designs to the public on the runway.

4

How would I describe my job to someone who wants to get into manufacturing? Well, first of all, it involves meeting often with our clients, who are mostly from the fashion industry, and talking about making their products. We provide a full service: sourcing the fabric and then cutting and sewing it according to the client's instructions. I spend a lot of time on the factory floor overseeing production making sure the job gets done, but my job also involves travelling a lot to trade fairs, sourcing new materials and making contacts.

5

This job has really transformed in the past 20 years. It's not just a desk job anymore, working for one editor.

These days, there are so many more opportunities to freelance, across a variety of media: print, online, TV, YouTube, and social media sites. We spend a lot of time doing research, or doing interviews, and mixing in our own opinions, too. I guess you could call us 'factual critics.'

UNIT 1, EXERCISE 8

M = Melissa, Designer,
S = Susan, Merchandiser,
E =Erika, Pattern maker

M   Right. Let's get started on our first review of the spring women's wear line. Susan, are you still working on the market research?

S   Really, it's just about finished. In fact, our results so far show that generally there is a positive response to our proposed line. But I'm not sure we can include all the styles if we want the collection to be profitable.

M   Really? How many do you think we can include?

S   Probably around 40 in total. It depends a little on the budget and on how efficient the pattern designs are.

M   I see. Well, the design team is still working on the casual line, so let's focus on the career line for now. Erika, do you have any suggestions for how to make the patterns more efficient? Shall we start with the pale blue suit?

E   Yes, lets do that. If we leave the collar and lapels off the jacket, it'll use less fabric and be quicker to sew. We can also reduce the number of buttons, from four to three.

S   That's a good idea, Erika. What about the other pieces for the suit?

E   Well, the blue trousers are a standard piece, so the hem, waistband and seams are no problem. For the white shirt, it depends on the number of design details. Melissa, what's your team thinking of including?

M   The team's working on bringing a fashion-forward look to our classical line. For blouses, we're including embroidered motifs on collars and cuffs, as well as for shirts. Shirts will also have an embroidered motif on the chest pocket.

E   Hmm, fewer details would mean faster production.

M   OK, well, I'll keep that in mind.

S   What about the outerwear coat?

M   You mean the navy blue one? We're going with four front pockets

and an oversized lapel.

S   I wonder how much extra fabric that translates into. We have to remember the budget, you know.

E   I think the production team is sewing a sample of the outerwear coat today. When that's finished, we'll know the exact quantity of fabric we need per coat.

S   OK, shall we look at which patterns we could cut ...?

UNIT 1, EXERCISE 12

M = Melissa, Designer
S = Susan, Merchandiser

M   Hello?

S   Hi Melissa. It's Susan from merchandising here. How's the research for the autumn/winter line going?

M   Really well. We're ready to give the line a name: *Blue Turkish Delight.*

S   That sounds fantastic. I can't wait to see the storyboard. How's it coming along?

M   Good. The design team is still researching different prints for the collection. We're trying to figure out whether to include geometric prints, as well as florals and paisleys. What do you think? Are people buying prints at the moment?

S   Definitely. More and more people are mixing prints with solid blocks of colour, and some people are even wearing clashing prints. It's definitely a growing trend. What colour palette are you using?

M   Well, the colour theme is turquoise and dark and light blue. We're also including some green tones, like teal and emerald.

S   Great, our clients will really go for those colours. They're becoming really popular.

M   Exactly, and people can also mix and match them easily.

S   Yeah, it sounds as if our customers will really like it. I look forward to seeing the finished storyboard at next week's meeting. Do you know what the PR department is planning for the line?

M   They're thinking of promoting the line by organizing a colour-themed event in-store, with models wearing the designs. Helen will be at the meeting next week and she's planning to talk us through the PR campaign then.

S   Great, well, I'm looking forward to it. See you at the meeting.

M   OK, see you then.

UNIT 2, EXERCISE 1

1
Before the 1750s women were mostly responsible for sewing and decorating clothing. In the 1840s, two Americans, Isaac Singer and Elias Howe, invented individual sewing machines. What did this mean for the fashion industry? The arrival of machinery during the industrial revolution meant that making clothes became men's work. In addition, the use of machinery led to mass production, which meant clothing became more available and affordable.

2
There didn't always use to be shopping centres where consumers could find everything they needed. Nowadays, department stores or online specialist retailers stock a big range of items of clothing and it's very easy to find things you need. But it used to take up a lot of time for consumers as they had to buy each item from a different vendor. So, when did this organization of selling and buying change? It was around 1840 in Paris when the first retail outlet decided to combine a variety of products in one store. Soon after, many stores started selling a range of fabrics, trim and embellishments and accessories.

3
When people think of fashion, they often think of France. But, it was an Englishman – Charles Frederick Worth – who is recognized as the father of the luxury fashion house in France. After moving to Paris, he started as an assistant in a dressmaking shop. A few years later, in 1857, the House of Worth was set up. He changed dressmaking by offering consumers new ways to buy clothes, like mix and match pieces, and by putting on seasonal shows for House of Worth's designs. Clients used to tell dressmakers how they wanted their clothes to look, but with the House of Worth, the designer basically decided which styles clients would wear.

4
Designers like Paul Poiret, Lucile, and la Maison Paquin used live parades of models walking around at shows to present seasonal collections for invited journalists and merchants. Lucile, in particular, used to give her shows themes, and she trained her models to walk in a special way and gave them exotic names. This interested the audience and started the lifestyle storyline that so many brands use today. Modelling at that time was not a profession, so actresses, opera singers and dancers used to walk the runways. Later, Elsa Schiaparelli produced theatrical themed collections and her shows – with music, dance and special lighting – attracted New York's high society.

5
Individual countries have always tried to promote their commercial strengths and in 1900, France hosted a global gathering of not only fashion designers and houses, but also merchants and inventors. The increasingly well-known couture houses did not miss the opportunity to display their creations, and they paid careful attention to the arrangement of their mannequins and sets. But next to the larger houses, small designers and shops could also show their creations. Today, fashion weeks offer similar opportunities to designers, from those at the very beginning of their careers to leading global brands.

6
After World War II ended in 1945, fashion played a major role in generating money and creating new business models. Couture houses reopened, and Dior launched the hugely influential 'New Look'. He presented it at the seasonal fashion shows in 1947, along with other designers, such as Jacques Fath, Hubert de Givenchy, and Gabrielle Chanel. These leading French designers licensed their names to manufacturers in the US, who produced more affordable clothing lines. Consumers bought the garments, along with accessories like handbags and sunglasses. It was profitable until the 1960s, when young people demanded street styles. As a result of that demand, labels had to become much more accessible and affordable.

UNIT 2, EXERCISE 9

V = Viviana, Historian, A = Andi, Interviewer

A … that's very interesting, Viviana. I'd like to go on and discuss the history of fashion illustration. Could you tell me more about the role of fashion illustration over the centuries?

V Of course. Well, you see, illustration has almost completed a full cycle. It used to be the most important tool for communicating styles to customers until it was almost completely replaced by photography, but now it's popular again.

A How did fashion illustration begin? Was it used for advertising?

V Not really. In the sixteenth century, illustrations were included in society papers at the French and Spanish royal courts. Some very good artists were commissioned to paint high society women wearing popular styles. Many were produced as engravings – you know, when they trace a design on something like copper and then transfer it to paper.

A I see. So when did illustration become an essential part of fashion promotion?

V It was Paul Poiret who first used illustration to promote his designs. He used to commission limited editions of artists' illustrations of his designs and publish them as albums. These albums were promoted as pure artwork, but they also brought customers into the atelier.

A That was about the same time that the fashion magazine La Gazette du Bon Ton was launched. Which illustration styles did that publication prefer to use?

V Many artists contributed to La Gazette du Bon Ton. Maybe two of the best known were Georges Barbier and Umberto Brunelleschi. They used to use wood blocks for printing, similar to the technique that is used in Japanese prints.

A How interesting! Much later in the 1930s, the photographic camera replaced illustration in fashion magazines. Was that the end of illustration in fashion?

V Well, historians have called it 'the death of fashion illustration' and Vogue and other magazines certainly preferred photographs to illustrations. But the fashion industry revitalized illustration in the 1980s and some innovative lifestyle magazines like i-D mixed it with photography in a dramatically modern way. It was as if illustration and photography had finally found a way to exist together.

A Are illustrations today found only in magazines?

V Oh no, actually, they are everywhere: in fashion magazines and as advertising campaigns as well. One famous department store in New York used illustration in an advertising campaign in the 1990s and it was very successful.

A And are the illustrations we see today very different from those in the early twentieth century?

V Absolutely! Today you can see all kinds of techniques used, from hand-drawn to computer generated. The important thing is that illustration continues to tell the story of fashion.

A Viviana, thank you for sharing your expertise with us. It's been fascinating to learn more about fashion illustration.

V You're welcome!

UNIT 3, EXERCISE 3

First, the raw materials have to be sourced from a range of international, or sometimes local, suppliers. Then they go through a series of refining stages. For example, the seeds and leaves in natural materials like cotton need to be removed so they don't go into the final textile. Next they are ready to be spun into yarn or thread on spinning machines. Once the yarn or thread is ready, the material is woven into fabric rolls. After that, the fabric may be coloured – either dyed or printed – and then finished, for example given a chemical treatment to make the fabric waterproof, say, for outdoor jackets. Finally, the fabric may be embellished or decorated, for example with embroidery or lace.

UNIT 3, EXERCISE 7

Here at FabriTex, we work hard to provide our customers with high-quality dyed fabrics for clothing and accessories. We have a range of chemical or plant-based dyes for customers to choose from.

Our eco-friendly range of organic dyes is made from pigments derived from plants, so the impact on the environment is minimal. They're all water-based with no chemical fixers, and come in a wide range of colours, including our signature indigo, a deep blue-violet colour. Unfortunately we can't guarantee colour fastness for the organic dyes, particularly with darker colours.

For colours that are guaranteed to last, our inorganic range is ideal. Chemicals are used to set the colour and we test all fabrics to ensure colour fastness. We want our colours to stay on the fabric, not on your skin! For pale or no-colour results we use a chemical bleach.

It's important to us to ensure your fabrics are comfortable, so we have a range of finishing processes to soften them, especially for denim, or for waterproofing.

We also offer special services such as embellishment – embroidery or appliqué, or resist dyeing methods with wax designs. There's also imprinting or wood blocking for your favourite graphics, and our highly trained pattern designers can help advise you.

Whatever your dyeing, embellishment or finishing needs, FabriTex delivers high quality and speedy service! Just visit to our website, or call us on our free phone number with any questions.

UNIT 3, EXERCISE 10

B = Buyer, S = Supplier

1
S Hello, and welcome to our stand.
B Good morning, thanks.
S Can I show you anything in particular?
B Well, my company is looking for some cotton knits for our summer line.
S You've come to the right place! We've got striped cotton jersey knits, polka dot cotton twill, and a cotton and poly blend, all of

which are available in a rainbow of colours.
B That sounds good. Could I see some swatches or samples?
S Sure, there're right over here …

2
B Hello, I see by your stand that you specialize in yarn.
S That's right. We produce a few types of synthetic yarns but most of our production is organic.
B Oh really? What kind of organics do you produce?
S Well, we've got sheep's wool, camel hair, alpaca, angora and some cashmere.
B Great, for our winter collection we're planning V-neck wool vests, tartan skirts and cashmere sweaters, so the yarns you mentioned are ideal. Are there any samples I can look at?
S Well, we have yarn samples but we don't have any sample garments.
B Oh, that's too bad. Can I take a brochure instead?
S Of course, here you go.

3
FD = Fashion designer, S = Supplier

S Can I help you find something?
FD Well, I'm looking for fabrics to inspire me for my fall and winter collection. I sell my designs in my own boutique and it's very important for me to use high quality fabrics.
S Are you looking for synthetic or animal-based fabrics?
FD Actually both. I'd like to focus on luxury, so anything that looks and feels like velvet, silk, leather and fur should work. My clients want clothes that are both glamorous and easy-to-wear, for example a black silk tank top or a velvet skirt.
S OK, we've got both synthetic and animal based fabrics for those examples. Here's a polyester-cotton blend that looks like velvet, and this is a silk-like fabric.
FD They look very interesting, but I'll have to see how they fall and drape on a mannequin.
S We have samples made up just for that purpose. There are some draped over there on the mannequins. Would you like to see them?
FD Yes, that would be great!

4
B = Buyer, S = Supplier

B Hi there.
S Hello. How can I help you?
B Well, I see from your sign that your company specializes in innovative finishings.
S That's right. We do everything from easy-care acrylics to wrinkle-free cotton to fabrics for breathable

activewear.
B What about waterproof finishes? Do you do them, too?
S Absolutely. We've got this new process that makes outerwear – I'm assuming you work for an outerwear company …
B That's right. I'm researching ways to make our jackets more waterproof and durable.
S I see. So, I was saying that our new waterproofing process, well, it does just that, but as well as waterproofing, it lengthens the lifespan of the fabric.
B Have you done performance tests? Could I see some statistics?
S Yes, we have. Let me just show you some recent test results on my laptop here …
B Right, oh, and do you have a sample I can take a look at?
S Of course, right this way please …

5
B = Buyer, S = Supplier

S Hi, can I help you?
B I'm just looking for now.
S Do you work for a clothing manufacturer?
B Actually my company makes raincoats and umbrellas.
S Oh, we do lots of business with outerwear companies.
B Really? We're currently looking for a new supplier for nylon and synthetic animal fur, like fake sheepskin.
S Oh, I'm sorry to say we don't supply anything like that.
B That's a shame.

UNIT 4, EXERCISE 6

1
A = Pattern maker 1, B = Pattern maker
2

A Have you got the specs for the new winter trousers?
B Yes, I've just put them into the system.
A Are we supposed to include a cuff?
B Yes, the design calls for a 7 centimetre cuff, but I'm not sure we'll have enough fabric. I'm wondering whether we should reduce it to 5 centimetres.
A Let's make two possible patterns and see what the CAD software calculates for the fabric amount.
B OK, that sounds good to me.

2
D = Designer, PM = Pattern maker

PM Hello.
D Josie, hi, it's Paul from Design Development.
PM Hi, Paul. What can I do for you?
D I just wanted to make sure you got the spec sheet for the coat.

PM Yes, I did. Was there anything you wanted to change before we start sewing the prototype?

D Actually, yes. Could you add another top pocket on the left front piece? I've ordered some extra material and it's on its way.

PM OK. I'll see that it gets put on and will let you know as soon as it's done.

D Great, thank you.

3
D = Designer, PM = Pattern maker

D Hi Susan. I came by to see if you've done the fabric layout on the sample cutter yet.

PM Hi John. Yes, I have.

D How's it looking?

PM Well, I'm not so sure this is the fabric we want for the shirt. Take a look at how the back yoke cuts.

D I see. Let's check the specs ... Here they are.

PM What do they say?

D Um, the body, sleeves and collar all need to be cut vertically, but the back yoke is cut horizontally. That should allow for more ease of comfort.

PM Oh, I see now. Sorry about that. I'll reprogram the sample cutter and try it again.

D Thanks.

4
D = Designer, PM = Pattern maker

PM Hi, Jen. Can I talk to you for a moment?

D Sure, Kate. What about?

PM Well, we put the design specifications for the Malibu skirt into the PDS and it's calculated that the extra fabric needed for the lining is over our budget.

D Really? That's not good news. We'll have to sew it without the lining.

PM Alright then, we'll revise the spec sheet as soon as possible. Thanks for letting me know.

5
PM = Pattern maker, D = Designer

D Is the prototype jacket ready for the style review?

PM Yes, our fit model is just putting it on. Here she is now.

D Great. Let's take a look and see how the fabric works 'live'. [to the model] Sara, could you please walk around and then sit in this chair?

D Thanks. What do you think?

PM The right top sleeve looks a little longer than the left one.

D You're right.

PM OK. I'll have to make the changes to the spec sheet. We'll let the left one out a bit.

D Sounds good to me. Let me know when the new prototype is ready.

UNIT 4, EXERCISE 10

PM = Pattern maker, D = Designer

D Are we ready? OK, well, to start with, I think we need to include bootcut jeans in this collection.

PM I agree – the pattern is quite basic. I think we should also remember that we can use a similar pattern for wide leg trousers.

D Yes, you're right. I'm just not sure that two wide leg trouser types would sell that well. Do you see what I mean?

PM Yes, maybe you're right. Should we go for a tapered trouser then?

D Well, let's think about that one for a moment. We can come back to it later. Moving on, which jacket patterns are we using?

PM It's a casual line so there's no space for a double-breasted jacket, right? It's too formal.

D Absolutely. I was thinking about including a cinched waist jacket. What do you think?

PM OK, but it'll use more fabric than a cropped one, so we'll have to see if we have the right amount of fabric after we put the specs in the CAD program.

D OK. Could you let me know about that, say, by tomorrow afternoon?

PM Sure, no problem.

D Great. Now, let's see ... Next we have shirts. I see from the specs that the shirt pattern allows for a lot of ease of movement. I'm not so convinced that winter is a time for loose fit shirts.

PM I see your point. We could easily modify it to make it more fitted.

D Would you have to take in a lot?

PM Probably not. I think we could do it by taking in about 3 centimetres.

D That sounds good. I'll draft a couple of designs after this meeting.

PM Great, once I have those I can start working on the new spec sheet.

D Sounds good. Now, we just need to go back and make a decision about the cut of the trousers. What do you think ...

UNIT 5, EXERCISE 2

QA = Quality assurance analyst,
S = factory floor supervisor

QA Let's get started, shall we? We're looking at the ladies' trouser today. I've completed my quality assessment of production and have highlighted some issues on the checklist. The first thing I'd like us to look at is the fastener: the zip was broken in about a third of the trousers.

S Hmm, that's a high rate of error. It must be a faulty batch of zips. I'll follow it up with our supplier.

QA Good, thanks. And, there were

problems with the pockets. On many pairs, the front pockets were sewn one on top of the other. Why do you think that's happening?

S It might be because we have new machinery. Our operators are still receiving training on how to use the new stand-up sewing machines. At the moment they're not always producing consistent results.

QA OK, so how about getting new operators to work side-by-side with more experienced on-the-job mentors? The mentors might help the operators understand the line sheet instructions better.

S Sure, that's a great suggestion. We can definitely do that. So, now that we've looked at the front pockets, what about the back pockets?

QA I'm glad you asked – on several pairs, the back pockets were left unturned before sewing.

S Hmm, it's difficult to say why that's happening but, again, I think that it might be a problem with the new staff. The group working on the back pockets will finish their training this week, so hopefully that will correct these problems.

QA I see, yes, let's hope so. Right, on to stitching problems... At times, there's irregular stitching and it makes the leg hem weak, which means one trouser leg is often longer than the other.

S Maybe we need to check the stitching more frequently. How about we send someone down to the sewing floor every hour to check on trouser hems?

QA I think that's a good idea, at least until we can identify the source of this problem.

S OK, I'll send you regular updates on that until it's cleared up.

QA That should also help with the final item on my list – the gaps in the side seams, which are due to dropped stitches.

S Hmm, I'm not quite sure how that happened. It must be a mechanical problem. I suggest we check that the machines are working correctly each day before we start assembling garments.

QA That sounds like a good action plan to me.

S Great. I'll include that information in my progress updates to you.

QA OK, let's hope we see a significant improvement soon.

UNIT 5, EXERCISE 8

M1 = Manager 1, M2 = Manager 2

M1 Well, I just got off the phone with the people from Nishao department store. I've got some more detailed instructions about how they want their garments packaged.

M2 Great. Did they say what they wanted to do about folding the men's shirts?

M1 Yes, they said they want the shirts machine-folded but not tagged, with cardboard and straight pins.

M2 OK, and did they say whether they preferred individual bags?

M1 Yes, they'd like them in separate plastic bags, with about 25 in each box.

M2 We can do that. How about the jeans order?

M1 Well, they told me they'd prefer hand-folding, and that all jeans should be delivered with hangtags.

M2 OK. And what about packaging?

M1 Yes, they'd like the jeans to be 50 per box.

M2 No problem, we can do that quickly.

M1 Oh, I nearly forgot. They told me to make sure that the jeans are packed with a piece of tissue paper in between garments.

M2 OK, that shouldn't be a problem. That just leaves the dresses …

M1 Yes they want the dresses in FRM form, so not folded.

M2 Oh, really? Then I guess we need to put hangtags on them too.

M1 That's right, and they also want us to hang all the dresses in rayon garment bags.

M2 Do you know what kind of hanger they'd like?

M1 Well, they said that they'd prefer fabric hangers since the dresses are delicate.

M2 Anything else?

M1 On the orders? No, but they said they enjoyed working with us.

M2 Well, that's a nice compliment! OK, let's get to work on those orders …

UNIT 6, EXERCISE 6
14

1

A The product line is for all end-users. There will be items for work, weekend, evening, day-into-evening and secondary bags, like laptop or work cases. The idea is that, as an accessory, we'll always be by your side just like a trusted friend.

B I see. Well, our top priority is to raise brand awareness. Any ideas for promotion?

A Well, first of all, with a small budget, we need to be creative. So, we're thinking of using flyers to attract more customers: they can be in the shape of our bags and we can distribute them near our stores. For this to be effective, we need a promotion printed on the back, say 10% off a purchase, with the flyer.

B That's a great idea, but it's also important to increase our brand recognition in a more general way. For example, we could create a

webzine where we talk about how our line has lots of modern looks, even trendy ones. And maybe this is less important, but our website can offer a 'view inside' option, so customers could almost experience holding our products in their hands.

A Those are all good ideas. Shall we see how they might work with the budget?

2

A This launch should be a memorable event, especially since we're doing it at the modern art museum. The artist Gillian Guilford has agreed to design the bottle, and the researchers are working to source new raw materials for the aroma. The purpose is to use the artist as a muse and as an inspiration for a truly unique scent.

B That's great! I'm so glad Gillian's going to be working with us on this project. So, our first priority for the marketing campaign is to link the fragrance with art.

A Yes, we should really promote the artistic connection.

B Another thing to consider is getting coverage in the fashion press.

A Why don't we get Gillian to do an interview?

B Well, she's quite shy, but I suppose she might agree to a written interview.

A That sounds good. We could put it on our website.

B OK, and we could also do a photo gallery of her at the launch party.

A Good idea.

3

A Our own brand of crockery is almost ready to launch, so can you talk us through the marketing strategy for the new line?

B Well, we have a photo shoot set up with the actress Mina Pantano. She's agreed to be the testimonial in our magazine ads. First and foremost, the goal is to get the customer to make a connection between her role as a TV mother and our crockery line.

C But don't you think that an actress with her reputation could distract customers from buying our products? She's had some bad publicity recently.

B Perhaps. Maybe we should wait and see how the photo shoot goes, but focus groups show that customers link TV roles to products.

A OK, I suppose we can give it a try. It should create a buzz, anyway!

B We also plan to do special in-store events, like demonstrations in the homewares dept. to show customers how good the line is.

A How about getting a well-known chef for those demos?

B Let's focus on the big picture for now. We can work out the details later.

4

A I've got some good news! Truman designs has teamed up with Harrington's Department Stores to handle the marketing campaign for a new line.

B Great! What's the product line?

A Intimates and loungewear for men and women.

B So what are our marketing priorities?

A Above all, with the advertising campaign we need exceptional photography for print ads and a great director for TV and online videos. The idea here is to increase brand awareness among 18- to 25-year-olds, and to emphasise the image of luxury that our brand represents.

B We could also do a behind-the-scenes video for our website offering our customers an exclusive look at the collaboration. We could call it 'Bedtime Stories' or 'Truman Tales', or something like that.

A OK, although to do that we'd need a video editor. We can also include the video on our Facebook page. What about Twitter? Could we create a viral campaign?

B What if everyone who likes us on Facebook or retweets on Twitter automatically gets entered into a sweepstakes to win free products? What do you think?

A Hmm, I'm not sure. Maybe the viral aspect isn't as important, but I like the behind-the-scenes idea.

UNIT 6, EXERCISE 10
15

S = Susan, T = Tomas, R = Rachel

S Right, so we all agree that our priority for LeeAnn Designs is to think of fashion week events. The question is, which promotional channels are we going to use? How about we begin by discussing ideas for events?

T Well, if I could make a suggestion: it would be a good idea to get a celebrity endorsement and have that person at an event. What about someone from the music or film world? Our focus groups showed that LeeAnn's customers spend a lot of their free time going to concerts or watching movies.

R I like that idea. How about a singer in a rock band? Better still, why not get several cool young musicians or actors involved?

T   Good suggestion. I like it.

S   I agree. And how about having a cocktail reception with the celebrities and inviting LeeAnn's business partners to attend, too?

T   That's a great idea. I'll get in touch with LeeAnn Designs and see who's on their contact list.

S   Is there anyone else we could invite to the event? I'd recommend including some loyal customers and influential journalists on the guest list.

R   That could become a pretty long list of names. Do we have the budget for, say, 200 people?

S   Actually, we do. LeeAnn Designs really wants to stand out from all the other events of fashion week.

R   Good, then I'd also suggest inviting some people from Sashay, you know, the company that developed the fashion show phone application? It's a really popular app.

S   I'm sorry, but I don't think that will work. It will take attention away from LeeAnn Designs.

R   OK, I guess you're right.

S   Moving on … Let's discuss other possible events for the week. LeeAnn herself asked for something that would surprise the public at fashion week. Any ideas on that?

R   Have we thought about organizing a flash mob?

T   Well, that might work, but we've never put one together before.

S   Don't worry … just organize it like an in-store event. But keep it as quiet as possible – the surprise element has the biggest effect on customers.

T   That's true. What about the location? How about in a park, maybe near the zoo?

R   I'm afraid I'm not very keen on that idea because little kids going to the zoo could run right into our flash mob.

T   You're right. How about doing it in a popular shopping street, say at lunch time when there will be lots of people around?

S   That sounds great, but I'll have to check with the city's permits department first. We don't want to break the law! I'll do that and get back to you. Great ideas both of you.

UNIT 7, EXERCISE 3

G =Gabrielle, Fashion producer,
A = Anita, Merchandise coordinator ,
F = Frances, Stylist

G   Let's get started, shall we? Last week we set the budget, so on the agenda this week are the show concept, publicity, the venue and the outfits. We'll also review who's

doing what. Anita, Frances, do either of you have anything to add?

A   Gabrielle, I think we should also discuss which modeling agency we're going to use.

G   You're right, Anita. Has anyone made contact with Estelle Agency yet?

A   I haven't done that yet.

F   I haven't either.

G   Well, I'd like you to handle that, Anita, and also please call Georges Models. We'll need to get both agencies daily rates to compare costs.

A   Sure, Gabrielle, I'd be happy to.

G   Great. OK, first on the agenda is the show concept. Could you both confirm that all the teams know about the seaside concept for the spring/summer collection? Frances?

F   Well, I still have to let the stage manager know.

G   OK, you'll have to let him know by the end of the week, Frances.

F   Right, I'll do that.

G   Anita, how about you?

A   I've informed most of the stylist team, but I still have to let Alex know.

F   Sorry Anita, who's Alex again?

A   He's the promotional coordinator.

G   That's right. OK, well, you'll have to tell him about the show concept by tomorrow, Anita. I'm meeting him the following day to talk through the budget for advertisements and invitations.

A   I'll do that right after our meeting today. Gabrielle on the invitations, are we going to send e-invites?

G   Yes, Anita, I'd like to. Please be sure to mention that to Alex when you speak to him later.

A   I will.

G   Moving on … How far have we got with choosing a venue?

F   Well, we've only had time to look at one place and it was too small.

G   Given how close we're getting to the show date, I think we need to make this a priority. Anita, you're going to help Frances to find a location by next week. Can you work together on that? Remember, we need somewhere near the river.

F   That sounds good. I've got a few ideas to follow up.

G   OK, do that and get back to me as soon as you have any news. Let's see … That leaves us with the last item on the agenda – the outfits. Frances?

F   Well, I've had a couple of meetings with the designer but we still need to agree on the final lineup.

G   Do you need help with that? I'll be free next Tuesday afternoon. See if you can set up a meeting with the designer for that day and we'll try to finalize the number of outfits for

the show.

F   That would be great, Gabrielle, if you could help me with that. Thanks.

G   No problem. It looks like the show is shaping up well so far. Now, before we finish, is there any other business …?

17

UNIT 7, EXERCISE 8

1   D = Director, A = Assistant

D   Let's get started on the dress rehearsal. Are all the models here?

A   Well, about that …

D   About what?

A   Unfortunately, not all the models have reported in.

D   What do you mean? It's in their contracts: they're supposed to be on time.

A   You're absolutely right.

D   So … have you tried to call them?

A   Well, not all of them filled out the contact information sheet, I'm sorry to say.

D   Really? Let's see what we can do to remedy the situation. Get on the phone to the modelling agency and have them email us the models' contact information, OK?

A   Right away. I'm sorry this happened.

D   OK, but we need to sort this out quickly. The show's in five days. So lets get on with it, yeah?

2   M = Manager, A = Assistant

M   Why do we have a Y-shaped catwalk?

A   Er…

M   The floor plan specifically called for a U-shaped one. Not everyone in the audience can see the models on the catwalk with a Y shape. Didn't the builders see the updated floor plan I sent out via email?

A   I'm terribly sorry. I take full responsibility for not telling them. I haven't spoken to the builders for a few days. I didn't realize they were working from the wrong plan.

M   You should be in contact with them every day. Well, I guess there's enough time to change things, but it's a time-consuming and expensive mistake.

A   I'm so sorry. It won't happen again.

3   D = Director, A = Assistant

D   Let's review today's progress before going home.

A   OK, let me just bring it up on screen…

D   Why is it taking so long?

A   Oh no…

D   What?

A   I hate to tell you this but it looks like I didn't save today's file.

D   What are we going to do now?

Didn't you make a back up copy?

A I usually do, but with all the changes with the stage construction yesterday I forgot. I'm so sorry.

D Don't worry. There's always another copy somewhere. Check your email.

A OK, checking now ... Oh, thank goodness! Here's a copy I emailed to the stage manager.

D Good, but from now on, make back up copies on your USB key and email me a copy every day, OK?

A I will. I apologize again.

4 FD = Fashion Director , D = Dresser

D I hate to tell you this but it looks like that model didn't get dressed on the floor covering.

FD Well, could you go over there and check to make sure the dress isn't dirty. That's the last thing we need.

D OK, I'll go check ...

FD Well?

D Er, it is a little dirty, but I don't think it will show as the dress is dark blue.

FD I suppose you're right, but we'll have to clean it before returning it.

D I'll see that it's cleaned. I'm so sorry. It was my responsibility to tell all the models about the floor covering.

FD OK, but you should remind all the dressers that the models have to stand on the floor covering while changing outfits.

D I will.

5 FD = Fashion Director, A = Assistant

A Uh-oh, what is Sasha doing out on the catwalk before Umi? I should go and tell the fashion director.

A I'm afraid to say that one of the models went out on the catwalk out of turn.

FD What? How on earth did that happen?

A Well, um ... I'm sorry but I think I was distracted and didn't double check the lineup sheet, so they didn't stay in the correct order.

FD I understand. Things can go wrong. Look it's only one model out of turn, so make sure you stay by the entrance and keep track of them for the rest of the show. And, please refer to the lineup sheet... both you and the models.

🔘 **UNIT 8, EXERCISE 4**
18

A = Allison, Visual merchandiser
S = Assistant, Stan

A OK. It looks like we've got everything. Could you dress the mannequins while I get the ladder?

S Do you need a hand with the ladder?

A No, thanks, I can handle it ... Right, I've got the ladder. How are

you getting on with dressing the mannequins?

S Great, I've just finished putting the accessories on them. Could you help me install the background panels?

A Yes, no problem. Would you pass me the stapler please?

S Here you are. Shall we staple the two panels together?

A All right ... there .... Great. Now, on to hanging the cloud props ...

S OK. Let's move the ladder over here. Can you hand me the screwdriver?

A Sure, here you go. The plan says they hang over the two mannequins, so I suppose one cloud goes over each mannequin.

S There, one of them is ready.

A Stan, how low can the other cloud go? What do you think?

S Well, I think it can go a bit lower. Just a moment. How does this look?

A That looks good.

S OK, let me just screw it in ... . Does this look OK?

A Yes, that looks about right.

S Right, what's next?

A Well, we've got the prop for the dog ... Is the female mannequin supposed to hold it?

S Just a moment ... I'm looking at the plan ... Uh, it says the dog is next to the tree prop.

A OK ... there we go. Right, the last two things we need to do are the lighting and the decals.

S I'll do the lighting if you stick the decals on the window.

A Sounds good to me, but are you sure you don't need a hand with the lighting?

S Well, just tell me how they look when I get them set up. OK?

A OK ...

S So, does the yellow spotlight work? I've angled it onto the female mannequin.

A Yes. That looks good to me.

S Then the other spotlight should be on the male mannequin. Could you take a look? Does this blue spotlight work?

A Hang on ... Yes, it looks fine. Stan, do you remember where the 50% off decal goes?

S Yes, it goes in the upper left hand corner of the window.

A Thanks.

S You're welcome.

A Now, I think we've earned ourselves a break. Shall we get some coffee?

S Yeah. that's a good idea...

🔘 **UNIT 8, EXERCISE 8**
19

B = Buyer, W = Wholesaler

B So, Joanna, we're very interested in some of the garments from your Spring ready-to-wear line.

W That's great news. What garments were you thinking of? Would you like to place an order?

B Well, I'd like to see what discounts you can offer us. How about we start with the skirts? What's the unit price on the brown linen skirt?

W 40 euros.

B If we order in high volumes, can you offer us a discount of say 20%?

W It depends – that's a pretty big discount. How many units are you thinking of ordering?

B Around 500 units. What would the cost price be per unit?

W Well, for that size order, I can give you a 15% discount on condition that you agree to a maximum of 10% buybacks. So, the price per unit would be 34 euros.

B Hmm ... 500 at 34 euros each, that's 17,000 Euros. I'm not sure we can meet that cost. It might be better if we reduce the number of units to 300 then. What's your best offer on an order of that size?

W OK. For that order type I can offer you a 10% discount, providing there are no buybacks.

B We could always discount the price in store sales, although I'd have to check with the head office before committing at this price.

W Actually, if it's an item you think you will stock across all your stores, I'll contact my supervisor and see what I can do. Let me call her. Do you think you could wait a few minutes?

B Sure, no problem.
(a few minutes later)

W OK well, I just got off the phone with my supervisor and she said that we could manage 35 euros per unit for the first400 units, and then 32 euros per unit for any orders above that.That's the best we can do.

B OK, that sounds fair. I think we have a deal. Oh, wait a moment,we still need to discuss delivery dates.

W We can usually deliver 4–5 weeks after an order is placed.

B Actually we need delivery within three weeks in time for our new seasonal promotion. Given that the order is a bit smaller, could you meet a shorter deadline?

W Hmm ... We can reduce the production time by a few days, but we can't speed up the delivery times from our Asian factory. Sorry, I'm afraid my hands are tied on this one.

B That's too bad. I think we may need to look at another garment instead. Is it a similar story for your men's knit sweaters?

W Well, ...

Useful phrases

UNIT 1

SPELLING –ING FORMS

With most verbs, add –ing
draw➔drawing, design➔designing, identify
➔identifying, try➔trying

With verbs ending in –e, delete the final –e and
add –ing
manage ➔ managing, source ➔ sourcing,
promote ➔ promoting

NB dye (which means 'colour hair or fabric')does not
lose the final –e:
dye➔dyeing

With short verbs ending vowel + consonant, double the
final consonant
fit➔fitting; plan➔planning

With verbs ending in –ie, change –ie to –y and add –ing
tie➔tying

DISCUSSING CURRENT PROJECTS

Asking about current projects
What are you working on at the moment?
How's (your project) coming along / going?
Are you looking into (using) different prints / fabrics?

Talking about current projects
I'm using (pleats) more and more.
I'm doing a lot of research / drawing / sketching.
We're trying to figure out how to (include more prints).
We're researching whether to (use geometric prints).
We're looking into (using fabric buttons).
We're working on (a new line).
We're ready to (give the line a name).
We're thinking of doing (a promotional event).
We're promoting the line with a fashion show.

Describing trends
(More and more) people are buying / wearing
(tuxedo-style trousers).
It's / There's a growing trend.
I'm / We're seeing this more and more.
It's becoming (really / very) popular.

UNIT 2

TALKING ABOUT PAST EVENTS AND HABITS

Talking about past events: past simple
Who (invented the sewing machine)?
How did (the first designers promote their styles)?
When did (this change)?
The second industrial revolution brought (new fabrics
to the fashion industry).
The couture houses didn't (miss the opportunity to
display their creations).

Talking about past habits: past simple & *used to*
Singers and dancers *used to walk /walked* the runways.
Tights *used to be worn /were worn* by men.
There *didn't use to be /weren't* any shopping centres.

We do not use *used to* to talk about past events.

DESCRIBING AND ASKING ABOUT ILLUSTRATION BRIEFS AND COMMISSIONS

Asking about illustration specifications
How (wide) would you like (the margins)?
How much (of the illustration) should include
(computer graphics)?
How (detailed / big) would you like (it to be)?
What kind of (techniques) would you like (to use) in
(the illustration)?
How will it be positioned on the page?
Should I make it ...?

Describing illustration specifications
It needs to ...
It has to / must / should ...
We would like it to ...
We want it to ...

PAST PARTICIPLES AS ADJECTIVES

Past participles can be used as adjectives to describe
trends or styles. Regular past participles are formed by
adding –ed to the infinitive:
mix➔ mixed
Many people today wear mixed looks: A tailored jacket
with ripped jeans and heels.

There are many irregular verbs:
wear➔worn
Many people like their jeans to have a worn look.
tear➔torn
He wore a torn shirt and black leather trousers.

UNIT 3

EXPLAINING A PROCESS

When we describe a process we often use passives:
Fabric *is made* from raw materials.

Explaining the sequence of a process
First / To begin with...
Second, / Then/ Next / After that,...
Before the fabric is (dyed), it is (woven).
At the same time,
Once /When the fabric has been woven, it is then (dyed).
Finally, / In the last stage,

WRITING CARE INSTRUCTIONS

Washing
Hand / Machine wash.
Wash with light / dark colours / separately.
Use mild detergent.
Dry clean only.

Drying
Tumble dry low/ medium / high.
Line dry.
Lay flat to dry. Reshape.
Dry the garment inside out.

Ironing
Iron on low / medium / high.
Steam iron.

Special Care
Do not wring.
Twist and knot.
Do not bleach.

REQUESTS, RESPONSES AND OFFERS AT TRADE SHOWS

Offering
Can / Could I show you anything (in particular)?
Can / Could I help you find something?
Would you like to see (some samples /swatches)?

Requesting
Do you happen to have any (velvet)?
Could / Can I see some (test results)?
Could / Can I have / take a look (at some swatches)?
Are there any samples (I can see / look at)?
Is there any way to see how it (drapes)?

Responding to requests
Sure, / Yes, / Of course, we've got some samples / swatches (right) over here.
Yes, let me just get (some more information / our pricelist).
I'd have to check with ...

UNIT 4

TALKING ABOUT PATTERN SPECIFICATIONS

Discussing specifications
Are we supposed to ...?
Do you think we need to ...?
Was there anything (you) wanted to change?
What does the spec sheet say?
This needs to be (cut horizontally).
We need to / We'll have to (add another pocket).
Look at (how the yoke cuts).
Let's see (how the fabric works).

Adjusting measurements
take (the leg) up (by 2cm) = make shorter
let (the hem) down = make longer
take (the waist) in = make narrower
let (the sleeve) out = make wider
allow for ease of comfort
take –cm off
add another –cm (around the shoulders)
centimetres, metres / inches, yards

UNIT 5

EXPLAINING CAUSES

it might be because + verb
it might be because of + noun
The holes in the seams *are due to* dropped stitches.
Since the stitching is irregular, the hem is weak.
It's difficult to say, but ...
it might/could/may be ...
it must be...

Explaining effects
The pockets were sewn differently so it looks like they are different sizes.
The hem is weak, which means (that) one trouser leg looks longer than the other.

REPORTING INFORMATION (INDIRECT SPEECH)

Asking what others said
Do you know what they want / wanted to do about + noun / gerunding?
Did they say whether / if they preferred ...?
Do you know what kind of ... they'd like?

Reporting what others said
They said / told me (that) they want / wanted ...
(Well,) they told me they'd prefer ...
They told me to make sure that ...
... they (also) want us to ...
They wanted to know if/whether we could ...

UNIT 6

EXPLAINING OBJECTIVES AND PRIORITIES

Explaining objectives
The idea is (that) …
The idea (here) is to …
The objective / goal / purpose is to …
The (launch) should be …, so …

Achieving objectives
For this to be effective, …
To do that, …
Another thing to consider is …
In addition, we can / could …
It's also important to …

Prioritizing objectives
Our top / first priority is …
First and foremost, …
Above all, …
Let's focus on the big picture for now.
Maybe this is less important, but …
Maybe … isn't as important.

MAKING SUGGESTIONS

If + I could …
If I could make a suggestion …

+ -ing /noun
I'd recommend / suggest …
What / How about …?
Have you thought about …?

+ verb
Why don't (you) …?
Better yet, why not …?
Let's …

RESPONDING TO SUGGESTIONS

Positive response
(That) Sounds good / great.
(That's a) Good / great idea.
Thanks for the suggestion.

Negative response
Well, that might work, but …
I'm afraid I'm not very keen on that idea.
I'm sorry, but I don't think that will work.

WRITING PRESS RELEASES

Audience: Press releases go out to news agencies, so write with this audience in mind. Ask yourself why journalists would be interested in reading about a person, product, service or event. Why is it newsworthy?
Title: Use active verbs (e.g. *announce, present, distribute, endorse*) in a present tense. Leave out articles like *a, an, the*: '*Sylista announces historic guest designer collaboration with UrikaWantabe.*'
Content: Explain essential information: Who? What? Where? When? Why? Use your company's name and the names of major participants and avoid personal pronouns (*he, they, it* etc.). You may even include a quote from someone important. Keep the tone formal.
Ending it: Write an effective conclusion. Leave your readers with a memorable idea.
Always include your contact information so journalists can ask for further information, if necessary. Finish with ENDS or - # # # -.
Read it before sending: Always read your press release before sending it. Look for common errors like: missing subjects and verbs; punctuation; wrong *–ing, -ed* or verb participle (*They're interested [interesting jeans]*; *We have been wear wearing them a lot.*);sentences that are too short (*It's a winner!*) or too long (*We're writing to let all stores nationwide and around the world know about our new, wonderfully smelling perfume that includes incredibly delicious scents such as cedar, rose, and musk, which were all found and created in our lab during the spring months last season*).

UNIT 7

DELEGATING AND RESPONDING

Delegating + verb
Can / could you + verb
I'd like you to (handle that).
you'll have to … by (the end of the week)
be sure to …
you're going to …
Can you work together on that?
OK, do that and get back to me …
See if you can …

Responding
(Sure), I'd be happy to.
(Right), I'll do that (when) …
(Yes / OK) I will.
That sounds good.
I haven't done that that yet.
I still have to / need to …

PROBLEMS

Informing About Problems
I'm afraid (to say/ to tell you) that …
Unfortunately,
I hate to tell you this but …

Apologizing
I (really) apologize for …
I'm (so / very/ terribly) sorry
I take full responsibility (for)….
It won't happen again.

Responding to Apologies
I understand. Things can go wrong.
OK. Let's see what we can do to remedy the situation.

(Well), we'll manage …
You should (be in contact with them every day).
OK, don't worry. / OK, but (from now on …)

UNIT 8

SETTING UP WINDOW DISPLAYS

Asking for and offering help
Could /Can /Would you hand /pass me …?
Could you help me?
Could you take a look?
Do you remember /know where …?

Do you need a hand with …?
Do you need help + –ing
Shall we ….?
Let's (move) …
Let me help you.
I'll do …, if you …

Responding to requests for help
Sure. Here/There you go/are.
Here it is.
I'd be happy to.

Asking and talking about how something looks
How does this look?
How high / low can this go?
Does this look (ok / about right / fine)?
Does this (lighting) work?

(That) (It) looks (good /fine).
That looks about right.
Put is so it looks like …

Negotiating
If we …, can/could you …?
What kind of discount can/could you offer on … ?
I'd like to see what discounts …

Proposing & offering conditions
I can … on condition that /provided that /providing /as long as …
We can't … unless …
Can you meet us in the middle?
How does (20)% sound?
Could you offer us a discount of …?

Responding to proposals
That sounds fair (enough).
OK, we can manage that.
I can /can't agree to that.

Keeping a position
I'm afraid my hands are tied (on this one).
I can't go any lower.
That's the best I can do.
Is that your best offer?

Delaying a direct answer
I'll see what I can do.
I'll have to think about it.
I'm not sure we can guarantee that.
I'd have to check with …

Confirming agreements
It's a deal.
Let's shake on that.
We have a deal.